What people are saying about The Core Method...

"Jim Shane's The Core Method is an emotional release technique that absolutely changed my life. I use it with all my clients and personally to release negative emotions and relieve stress. It has helped me purge some of my most bottled up negative attitudes and conceptualize a brighter future for myself, as well as inspired me to take action to pursue it. "

OH Georgia

"Jim's system was an awesome surprise. It worked so quickly and effectively. I have learned many different processes over the last decade, and they each have something powerful to teach me. What Jim has created cuts to the chase. It may be one of the first processes that I can physically 'feel' working through my body. Please put aside any preconceived expertise on how things are 'supposed' to work and experience this at face value."

JL Arizona

"I have been working with the CORE process for a number of weeks now. It has been incredibly helpful in releasing unwanted emotions. Whenever something bothers me, I use the method and within moments a warm flood, that feels like a wave washes over me and it is gone. The reason that these results are so incredibly extraordinary is that some of the abuse issues have been causing paralyzing fear and sickness for more than 20 years. I have tried prescription medication, therapy, different healing modalities and nothing has worked. Yet within a short period of time and practice, I have been able to become totally free of these issues. To say thank you doesn't seem adequate. This process has literally changed my life and restored me. Thank YOU so much for sharing your time, talents, and energy. You are a blessing. With love and gratitude. "

HP Arizona

"The CORE Method is such an incredibly useful and pragmatic tool. The concept is so simple it could easily be disregarded but the power of the method lies in the simplicity and accessibility of the method in daily life. Since discovering the CORE Method dramatic shifts have taken place in my life. Where I was previously challenged in circumstances now I take a breath visualizing the emotion at my root and allow the challenge to rise out of my body through the top of my head leaving me more clear, lighter, and ready to continue my day. The incredible improvements that can be gained in a matter of seconds cannot be understated!"

MB Wisconsin

"I asked Jim for help because of a trauma from 4 years ago. Energy had been stuck in my lower abdomen, in the 2nd chakra "creative space," leaving me unmotivated and insecure, unable to move forward in my life. With this process, the negative emotions just lifted right out of me and I was left in a very free and high space. Voila! A friend told me, "Wow! Your energy is so clear and lively!" In the next 2 days, I joyfully spent over 20 hours creating a video to launch my new work. I look forward to seeing even more results from daily practice!"

KG Arizona

"It's been about a year and I realized how the quality of life really improved using this method. When I first started in Jan. 2019 I was always triggered about my financial situation, bills would trigger me and I couldn't even look at my bank account. When I was introduced to this method instead of avoiding my triggers I took a deep dive, feeling my anxiety and panic and using the method. It wasn't long before I started feeling a sense of calm, unbothered about my situation. I looked forward to using the method in all situations so I began to feel even thankful for things that triggered me because I really felt like I was healing and recreating my life situation. I cleared so much emotional baggage I was able to see money differently and align to a better situation. I'm now only working 2 days a week at a job I love getting paid twice as much, I feel free. I can't remember the last time I've stressed about money or bills. I have more than enough even through this 2020 *pandemic. I'm still using the method now focusing more on my relationships and heart health. I'm so appreciative of Jim teaching this easy to use self healing tool."*

LS Kansas

"I finally had a good night's sleep and woke up relaxed. I have been using what you taught me this morning and I am amazed at how quickly I can feel better. It feels so strange to have thoughts pop up in my head and to feel next to nothing or even nothing about them. I have spent so long having gut punch reactions to things, that feeling good or even neutral about it feels strange. I hope to see you again sometime!"

LT Arizona

Hi Jim, You know me for being a spiritual and positive person. No matter what is "bothering" me, I have a tendency to always put others first. It is that service spirit that I have. Recently I have been struggling a great deal with whether or not to retire from ever working as a nurse again. Give up my license and just be at ease with whatever is to come. This has come to me in phases and I keep hanging on. However, I used your techniques along with what has been tried and true for me over the years and the way was so clear. I finalized my decision and I mailed my license to the state and I am not going to be a practicing RN any longer, I am retired. Does that mean that I am no longer a healer? No. This has allowed me to open other doors to being and your program has helped me be comfortable with those decisions and have no anxiety about it whatsoever. Thank you so much for sharing this part of yourself with me.

KW Maine

...read more testimonials to this work at the end of this book

Living A Life Of
Authentic Magic

Using
"The Core Method"

Living A Life Of
Authentic Magic

Using
"The Core Method"

Jim Shane

Copyright © 2020 Jim Shane
All rights reserved.

No part of this publication may be reproduced or transmitted in any form, or by any means, mechanical or electronic, including photocopying and recording, or by any information storage and retrieval systems, without permission in writing from the author. (Exception: A reviewer may quote brief passages in a review.)

Please be advised of the following: The information contained in this book, on any related social media, and resulting communications is educational in nature. It is provided only as general information, and should not be taken as medical or psychological advice. Transmission of the information presented is not intended to create a client practitioner relationship between Jim Shane or any of his associates. These teachings should not be relied upon as coaching, spiritual, medical, psychological or other professional advice of any kind. Always seek the advice of your physician or other qualified mental health provider with any questions you may have regarding a medical condition or mental disorder. Never disregard professional medical advice or delay in seeking it because of something you have read in this book.

Author: Jim Shane
Cover Design, Layout, Formatting, and Content Editing:
Andrea King www.flowganize.com

Dedication

This book is dedicated to the Magic of the human spirit.

Contents

A Note From the Author	13
"The Peoples"... A Personal Message	15
Introduction	17
Part One..	**35**
1. Identity... Who Are You, Really?	37
2. The Invisible Secret of Life	39
3. A Reality Check About Your Choices	43
4. You Have Everything You Need to Make Huge Changes to Your Life	45
5. Changing the Elements of Your Identity	49
6. The Incredible Impact of Your Emotions	53
7. The Significance of These Kinds of Changes	55
8. The Power of Authentic Magic. This is The Core Method	57
Part Two..	**59**
9. Creating a Foundation	61
10. The Plot Thickens	65
11. Two Main Elements of The Core Method	67
12. The Four Systems of the Core Which Make The Core Method Possible	71
Part Three..	**75**
13. Specific Core Method Elements	77
14. The Emotion Connection	81
15. Every Problem In Life Has Two Parts	85
16. Your Two States - "Wanting" and "Having"	89
17. Why Negative Emotions Exist, What They Mean and How The Core Method Deals With Them	93
Part Four..	**97**
18. How to Do The Core Method	99
Identify the Story	99
Feel the Intensity Level	99

Focus on the Emotion	100
Define What's Missing	100
The Three Questions	101
Experience Your Core	103
Doing The Core Method	105
The Core Method Review	107
Bad Habits	108
19. Techniques to Empower The Core Method	111

Part Five... 117

20. Other Important Concepts	119
21. Secondary Gain	123
22. An Interesting Secret About Your Emotions	127
23. Metaphors for The Core Method	129
24. Disapproval? Beat Yourself Up! This Equals Self Destruction!	133
25. The Three Hidden Qualifiers	139
26. The Core Method and the Power of Your Beliefs	145

Part Six.. 149

27. Knowing What to Let Go Of is Crucial to Your Magic	151
Attachments and Aversions	152
Resistance	153
Karma	154
Waiting For The Other Shoe To Drop	157
28. Closing Notes	159
If You do The Core Method and Don't Notice a Change	
The Magic Of The Core Method... Emotional Release!	162
My Three Rules of Life	163
Authentic Magic	165

About the Author
My Story of the Healing Hand
Resources
Stay Connected

A Note From the Author

Something to think about...

Life.

It's full of highs and lows. I like to refer to them as Magic and misery. Magic being the good times when life is truly worth living. Misery being the not so good times when you might even wonder if it's all worth the effort anymore.

Ever hear the old phrase, "Misery loves company?" It's true. People who are suffering are attracted to anyone willing to listen to their stories of struggle and pain hoping someone will care and empathize.

But there's also the Magical side of life. The happy side, full of people who are doing well and enjoying their lives.

Most people who are having a great time and enjoying life tend to want to share the fun with others, right? Family, friends and people of like mind. For these people, I've got a new one for you...

"MAGIC LOVES COMPANY!"

Now, I know Magic comes in many forms depending on who's watching, but the Magic I'm most interested in goes like this...

What if you had a way to change who you are? A way to affect your "identity" and become someone else? Someone different. What if you could create a better version of yourself and as a result, live a better life? A Magical life?

What changes can you imagine for yourself that would make your life amazing? Less worry and stress? More success and money? More free time? Better health? Great relationships?

What if these things began to work out for you... as if by Magic?

What if there was a way to make it all happen? What if you could finally begin to live your dream life?

The Core Method offers exactly this. A way to live a life of Authentic Magic. It began to happen to me as I applied the method to my life and in helping others. And it got better and better.

This is why I hope you'll take what you learn in this book seriously. Maybe even tell me your stories of success. It's always exciting to hear how someone has changed their life for the better with the method. Because like I say...

"MAGIC LOVES COMPANY!"

"The Peoples"... A Personal Message

Many years ago when I was around 30 years old or thereabouts, I got talked into joining Amway. If you don't know what that is, it's a network marketing company that sells just about everything. They started out in 1959 selling soap. Why? Because soap sells. At least that's what I was told.

Anyway, I got in and was soon told I should get in on their "tape of the month club". At the big Amway conventions, successful people would get up and speak to inspire the masses to go out and build the business. When the Diamonds and Double and Triple Diamonds spoke, these speeches were recorded because they were particularly inspiring. That's because many of these people were "living the dream" making tens if not hundreds of thousands of dollars a month.

When you read the introduction in this book, you'll learn how I discovered I wanted to be able to help people heal from their pain and emotional suffering in life. That'll help you understand where I'm headed here. One of the first Amway tapes I got was called, "The Peoples". Hmm. OK? I popped the cassette into my tape player and listened.

The man began telling the story of how he struggled in the business but finally succeeded. Along the way, the business made it possible for him to be able to help a lot of other people change their lives for the better too. That idea seriously impressed me because in my heart, I also wanted to help people change their lives for the better. I just wasn't sure Amway was the way I wanted to do it. That clarity would come later.

As he got deeper into his emotional story of struggle, he spoke with a quivering voice. I could imagine he had tears in his eyes. He referred to the people he helped along the way as "The Peoples". With all his focus, determination, dedication and hard work in supporting his business partners in their dreams of freedom, he made it clear that these "Peoples" were better off because he came into their lives. He was challenging his audience of business builders to care enough to make a difference.

I don't remember his exact words and I can't do his story justice, but near the end as he spoke, this is the question he put to his audience… "The Peoples"… will they be better cause you came?"

That question hit me like a 20 pound sledge hammer. Meaning I took it very personally. To me, this meant… will anyone be any better off 'cause I spent time on God's green earth? Will it matter that I was here? Will I leave behind anything good, or will I just leave?

By the end of his speech, I was in tears too. This question touched me so deeply that now, 40 years later, I still hold that thought in my mind as a benchmark of my time on God's green earth.

In learning all that I have, in helping people along the way and now in writing this book, I feel in my heart that the time I've spent here has been worth it. This book is my legacy. It will help many more people than I could by myself, even long after I'm gone.

I know what it's like to suffer. And I know what it's like to heal. It is my hope that the knowledge in this book will help you as it has helped me.

With my blessings,
Jim

Introduction

The Day It Started For Me

It was summer, 1963.

I was 12 going on 13 in August that year. I was at my friend's house. His mother asked him to run an errand for her at the library here in Mesa, AZ. He told me what's up, so we jumped on our bikes and headed downtown.

Once there, he went to the front desk to take care of business for his mom.

And me? I wandered aimlessly through the tall shelves of books waiting for him to finish. I mean, it was summer. I was 12 years old and school was out. Reading was the last thing on my mind.

To me, everything on those shelves was a mind numbing beige. Who cares?

At least that's what I thought. Until… I almost passed this one book.

It stopped me in my tracks.

Just above eye level on my left, it was bright yellow with a shiny cover. The back binding said in big, bold, red and black letters…

"TNT – The Power Within You!"

My first thought was, "The power within me?" That definitely got my attention.

I pulled it down from the shelf and looked at the cover. I saw the author's name, Claude M. Bristol, then cracked it open.
I scanned the contents and flipped some pages. I read a paragraph here, another there.

After a few more of those, I shut that book and took it straight to my buddy at the front desk and said, "Check this out for me! I want to read it!"

He did and I did... in about three days. A record for me! Ha!

Life Is The Greatest Teacher

Like so many people, I came from a broken home too.

Dad struggled to make a living. He was also gone most of the time. When he was around, it was rarely a good experience. He taught me at a young age that I was worthless. The thing is, I didn't realize that I came to believe him. By the time I was eight years old, he was gone. Divorce.

Mom, on the other hand, was great! She was always there for me. But like me, mom had a low self image too. While she would encourage me to think I could do anything with my life, she didn't know how to set an example I could believe in.

For the most part, my parents and the people we knew were rarely what you would call "successful" in life. I was surrounded by what most might call "mediocre" people.

Not even average people. More like the struggling masses. And that's who we were.

That was my model for how to be human. Just getting by and never really achieving anything.

By the time I was twenty years old, I had lived in twenty-one different places! At least the ones I can remember, which doesn't include the ones before I was two years old.

I was born into a vagabond existence with people who didn't know how to make life any better than struggling just to get by. I didn't realize it, but I was starving for information like that TNT book had in it.

Looking back, I've come to realize life experience has been my real teacher. In my 70 years on this planet, I've had enough to know a thing or two about what I call the "human condition".

I've seen the lowest dregs of human life to the greatest happiness and it's all taught me that my mom was right. Anyone and everyone has within them the ability to be, do and have anything they choose. It all comes down to one thing...

Who and what we believe we are... our "identity".

Your "identity" is made up of the many things you believe are true about you. But what if you stopped believing the same old things? What if you changed what you believe about yourself and the world? Would you still be the same person?

Is there something you believe about yourself that's keeping you from succeeding? From moving forward? From finding happiness and success? Change that belief and you change your "identity". Change your "identity" and you change your life. It's that direct.

My Path To The Core Method

Over the many decades since that day at the library, I've enjoyed over five hundred self-help, and self-improvement books.

I've read old classics like Think and Grow Rich, The Magic of Believing and Psycho-Cybernetics. I've also read newer books like The Power of Now, The Secret, and Urban Shaman. I've explored witchcraft, metaphysics, psychology, spirituality and much more.

I've been through dozens of seminars and life transforming experiences. The Lifespring training which came out of EST, (Erhard Systems Training's), a ropes course high up in the trees in the mountains of Utah, and Silva Mind Control in Phoenix, to name a few.

I've gone through hypnosis training and become a certified hypnotherapist. I've also gone through NLP training. (Neuro Linguistic Programming)

I've walked on fire with Tony Robbins. I even learned to talk to my body with a pendulum and then later I learned to do it through Kinesiology (muscle testing the strong/weak response).

Then I taught these things to others.

I've learned a dozen different techniques to make changes in a person's life. To name a few:

- Release Technique
- Sedona Method
- BSFF (Be Set Free Fast)
- Art Of Neutrality
- Emotion Code
- EFT (Emotional Freedom Techniques)
- ECC (Emotional Complex Clearing)
- Now Healing
- Reality Transurfing
- and more...

Over the decades, I've applied all I've learned to myself because like most people, I needed the help.

I've worked with hundreds of individuals, taught many classes in my favorite techniques, discovered my niche in energetic psychology and finally assembled my own method from all that I've learned.

I call it The Core Method. Using this method is how I began to experience what it's like to live a happier, more free life. A life of Authentic Magic. Now I want you to have this amazing method.

My First Exposure To Energetic Psychology

In 1988, when I was living in San Diego, Ca., I saw a successful psychologist named Dr. Roger Callahan on a TV ad.

He had developed an amazing way to overcome negative emotions "quick and easy" called Thought Field Therapy or TFT.

He was going to reveal it for $100 per ticket in his high rise office in downtown San Diego. I was excited to go!

I went and listened intently, but the whole evening was vague to me. There was a lot of confusing talk about energy and something about a European connection that I didn't understand.

I couldn't make heads or tails of what he talked about. I just didn't get it. So at the end of the meeting during Q&A, I raised my hand.

I asked him to explain it so I understood exactly how it works.

His response?

"You think I'm going to just give the whole thing away for a hundred bucks? It took me years to develop this!"

Wow. I left there with just enough information to embarrass myself the first time I tried it on someone. And that was that. At least for the time being.

Ten years later, here in Mesa, I was at work. I happened to turn on my favorite local alternative radio station and tuned into the middle of an interview.

The man was talking about something familiar. Something I tried to get long ago, but missed. He was talking about Dr. Callahan's method... TFT!

The man being interviewed was Dr. James V. Durlacher and he had written a book about TFT called, "Freedom From Fear Forever"!

What's more, his book was for sale in his office which was not 20 minutes away! After work, I raced over, met Dr. Durlacher and bought his book, autograph and all!

I Discover Voodoo!

Like the TNT book I read as a kid, I was excited to have this book and so I read it in just a few days. As I did, my focus was mainly on the actual technique of the release because it seemed quite complicated with all the testing points and release points and how they correlate.

But as I read, I also noticed that it said the method works on many physical problems too. That really caught my attention because for about 6 months or more, I had a real problem with cold sensitivity on my teeth.

I avoided eating anything cold on one side of my mouth because it was excruciatingly painful on my lower jaw.

This book was saying this method might help. I thought, "How is this possible?"

So there I was, alone at work.

It was lunchtime and the other guys were gone. I had my book, my chips, a cold-cut sandwich with iceberg lettuce, cheese and tomato, and a frosty cold drink, all right out of the fridge.

I read through the protocol once more as I thought about my sensitive teeth. And I wondered... Is this possible?" I decided to try it.

I set the book down. I set my sandwich down. It was my first time with that method.

I applied the protocol once. Only took about 30 seconds, so just to be sure, I did it again.

Once done, I picked up the cold sandwich and with serious trepidation... I took a bite.

I was hesitant to chew on the sensitive side so I was slow to move it over there. But when I did, just a little bit, it was no problem.

Hmmm.

I swallowed and almost felt a little emboldened. So I took another bite. This time, a BIG bite right out of the middle and just went straight for the pain!

I put that bite right on the sensitive side and chewed hard and fast...

Aaaaand... NOTHING!

No pain! Not a SPECK of pain! It was like it never existed!

WHAAAAT?!? My eyes got really big! I was in shock! Totally incredulous! Six months or more of sheer pain and suffering... gone in one minute! I swallowed, looked around and said right out loud...

"This is Voodoo!!!"

I started laughing hilariously! The cognitive dissonance I was experiencing had just tossed my brain right out the window! I was absolutely stunned!

After a minute or so, I recovered somewhat and just sat there shaking my head wondering, "How is this possible?"

As you might imagine, being interested in changing myself and helping others, I was HOOKED! I believed I had found the Holy Grail of self-improvement! I had found REAL MAGIC!

Nowadays, when I say Magic, I'm referring to what I call "Authentic Magic". Things I've learned that can be done by the natural human spirit. Every human being has the natural born ability to bring about very real changes to their life experience. You just need the right understanding and tools.

I got the name, "Authentic Magic" from a book I read by Dr. Wayne Dyer some decades ago. A story he told set that thought in my mind and the concept has been with me ever since.

I don't even remember the title of the book now, but after my experience at lunch that day, I now had an experience and method to make Authentic Magic REAL in my life!

My Family Gets The Treatment

This voodoo thing I learned was still brand new to me. I hadn't said anything to anyone about it yet. I wanted to experiment more.

A couple of days later, my wife and I had been discussing (arguing about?) something. I don't remember what. That night when we went to bed, more was said. It didn't turn out well for either of us.

Emotions were still tense so we both just laid there on our own sides of the bed stewing. After several minutes of silence, she got up to use the bathroom while I laid there all grumpy.

Suddenly I remembered this voodoo Magic thing I learned from Durlacher's book. I had been hesitant to try in on anyone 'cause I wanted to make sure it wasn't just all in my head.

So right there in bed, I applied it to myself... and suddenly, I was in a better mood! I was immediately relaxed about our little tiff! I instantly went from frustrated to fascinated by what I just did to myself!

Then she came back and got in bed. It was quiet "over there" for a few seconds. I took a chance and said I knew a way to help us feel better about this thing we disagreed on.

I told her I had just done it and it helped. She told me later she could tell by my voice and demeanor I was different.

But in that moment, I was different enough that she opened up and said, (with a bit of disdain) "What is it?"

I began to explain. And as weird as the method sounded, she miraculously let me do it to her. On a night where we would have gone to sleep all grumpy at each other and woke up that way, we were cuddling within five minutes. Magic!

Around that time, my oldest daughter was about thirteen, going through puberty, and let me tell you, the hormones were raging!

One day, she was in her bedroom laying on the floor just crying her eyes out. Her mother went in to try to console her, but with no success. She came out and asked me if I wanted to try that "thing" on her.

I was a little surprised, but I said, "Sure".

She went back in and asked my daughter, then came out and said she had agreed.

I went in and helped her off the floor and sat her on the edge of the bed with me. Then I asked her what she was feeling.

With tear filled eyes she said, "Confused and frustrated."

I asked which one was the most.

"Confused."

I explained the process in a minute or so and then took her through it. It only took about thirty seconds. Then I watched.

She immediately calmed down and got quiet. Her face softened and went smooth.

Her eyes opened and I asked, "How do you feel?"

After a moment, she looked right at me and said, "Really clear!"

She smiled brightly and gave me a BIG hug! Magic!

One night, another younger daughter had left her shoes out back under the trampoline. It was dark out and she needed to bring them in so they wouldn't get wet. I sent her out to get them but she came back crying and without the shoes. I asked her what was wrong.

She said, "It's dark out there! I'm afraid!"

I sat her on the porch swing with me and took her through the process. Then sent her to get her shoes. This time she came back in with them.

I said, "Was it so bad?" She said, "I guess not." Ha! Magic!

My Friends Get The Treatment

There were many occasions when I was able to help my family with this amazing new ability. Then my friends were getting it too.

I helped three women overcome migraine headaches. It was interesting to learn they were all connected to old anger. I used muscle testing to discover this.

I helped an older gentleman with headaches from the perfumes women wore at church. The method made it better and he went back.

In another incident, I helped a couple in two different ways.

After a pretty bumpy fender bender they were in together, she would flinch with fright at every little movement around her while in the car with him. I did the method on her and it was gone. No problem!

He had a painful memory from WWII. PTSD that he had never dealt with. He tried to tell me about it but started to tear up.

I stopped him and took him through the method. Within a minute, he was able to tell the whole story and was shocked he could do that without crying.

Then there was a bookstore owner with a painful childhood memory. As I guided her through the method, she sat there feeling the changes moving through her body. She was so excited to be able to think of all that and not feel the old sadness.

I even helped a new musician friend with stage fright. He was really nervous. He was about to go on stage and play a new song. I took him through the method backstage and he went on and played without a hitch.

There were SO many more I worked with and was able to help. I could go on and on. As this was happening, I even began teaching classes on the method.

During this early time in my education and being aware of Thought Field Therapy, I also discovered Emotional Freedom Techniques or EFT.

Gary Craig had taken TFT and simplified it and this is what I mainly used and taught. It was very effective on so many things. I have many wonderful memories of helping others with it.

But EFT and TFT were both very overt methods that required a lot of physical tapping on points of the body to produce the changes. In the back of my mind, I wished I could somehow get the same results without having to do anything people could see. I wanted a covert way to make the changes.

Little did I know my focus on that thought would one day be realized.

My First Experience Of The Core And Kinesiology

Ever open and willing to learn all I could about this kind of healing, in 1999 while living here in Arizona, I learned of Dr. Brad May in San Diego who had his own method of healing difficult emotions. He calls it Emotional Complex Clearing or ECC. He was hosting a training so I drove over to San Diego to go through it with him.

It was such an amazing experience for me that he put before and after preview videos of his work with me on his website. He has many such videos there.

Part of his training included Kinesiology or muscle testing. This was my first real exposure to this amazing way to talk directly to the subconscious mind through the body. I highly recommend you go on YouTube and learn this valuable skill.

Discovered back in the 1960's by Dr. Goodheart, muscle testing helps you get right at the heart of a problem in minutes or even seconds. This is what replaced swinging my arm like a pendulum to try to get answers.

I actually started with a pendulum in the early 90's and had progressed to just using my arm. But that was a slow way to get answers because I had to wait for the pendulum or my arm to start moving. Muscle testing is a more instant way to get answers.

When I say "my first experience of the core", I'm talking about Dr. May's method in San Diego. I didn't know it at the time, but there were others I would eventually learn from who had also discovered the power of the core of the body.

My Knowledge Grows

I learned both TFT (Thought Field Therapy) and EFT (Emotional Freedom Techniques) in 1998. The connection was easy because EFT came from TFT. But being open to energetic psychology set me on a path to more discoveries in this field.

The next year, 1999, I learned ECC (Emotional Complex Clearing) which directly employed the core of the body. I don't know if Dr. May would necessarily explain it that way, but from the path I took to my Core Method, the connection was quite clear to me.

Also around this time, I went through hypnotherapy training. I was glad to have that experience and did some successful work with it like helping a guy stop his constant hiccups, helping a woman stop smoking and another lose weight, etc. But ultimately I still preferred energetic psychology.

Around 2010, I discovered Dr. Brad Nelson's "Emotion Code". And I noticed he employed the core of the body basically the same way Dr. May did in his ECC. I found this very interesting but still did not have the whole picture yet.

During this time, I also learned the Release Technique and the Sedona Method. Both of these methods came from one man, Lester Levenson, a physicist and entrepreneur of the mid 20th century.

There were some very useful parts of these methods that I liked so later, I incorporated them into my method. But I really preferred the core work of the other methods so I tended to go that direction. EFT and TFT both required the outer physical tapping that if done in public, might seem a bit strange to others.

So I was always on the lookout for a more covert method to do the same inner work. Something I could do anywhere, anytime and no one would know I was doing it.

Then, around 2012, I bought a book by Jason Mangrum called "Uberman - Almost Superhuman". It's an amazing book filled with almost magical things that are possible for the human condition.

One chapter stood way out for me. It was Chapter 2 - "The Magic Of Centering Yourself". This is where the magic of core work began to come together for me. It totally related to my experiences with Dr. Brad May and Dr. Brad Nelson.

In 2013 as I researched this core work thing, I discovered Paul Wong and his "Art Of Neutrality" which closely followed the chapter 2 material in Uberman.

After going through Paul's training in The Art Of Neutrality, I discovered Elma Mayer's "Now Healing". Then I discovered that the basis of both Paul and Elma's methods came from Kam Yuen and his "Yuen Method". Kam is a 35th generation Shaolin Master.

Over the next couple of years, I began to realize the connections between all these methods. TFT, EFT, ECC, the Emotion Code, Release Technique, Sedona Method, the centering method described in Uberman, the Art Of Neutrality, Now Healing and the Yuen Method. In 2015 it all began to gel for me.

I took what I felt were the best parts of all these different protocols and assembled them into what I now call "The Core Method".

It's the simplest and easiest method I know of to bring about changes to one's beliefs, emotions and "identity" in seconds and help people live a life of Authentic Magic. And... it's "covert".

The Concept Of "Authentic Magic"

What is it?

Authentic Magic is what you experience as a result of regularly using The Core Method to clear the blocks to the flow of Magic in your life. These blocks show up in the form of negative emotions, judgments, beliefs, attitudes, opinions, etc.

Clearing them sets your vibration or frequency higher and higher which improves the quality of your life. Your state of being or "identity" gets lighter and lighter. This results in what I like to call "clarity of the human spirit".

This not only makes for a greater ease of life but also helps you attract what you choose. It becomes easier and easier to manifest wonderful things, people and experiences on purpose or even randomly.

In that state or as this new "identity", you'll find you live life in a more natural flow where struggle and pain are rarely or no longer necessary. And where they do occur, they are handled more easily.

"Self love" now sets the stage of life where things tend to work themselves out because fighting, resistance and struggle are rare. And where these might be felt on occasion, one quickly becomes aware and can release them with The Core Method.

- Goals come to fruition with greater ease
- Relationships of "every kind" become a blessing
- Health improves
- Success and prosperity come more easily
- Life flows more smoothly and is more enjoyable

Quite often, the deeply important things of life seem to fall together as if by Magic. Just know that this all comes in degrees. The more clear the spirit, the greater the Magic. Using The Core Method is how the spirit becomes clear.

Let me define "Clarity of the Human Spirit"

Life can get pretty hectic. It can weigh us down. Consider all the things that can demand your attention:

- responsibilities
- relationships
- meetings
- expectations
- career or work
- money concerns
- time limits
- rushing here and there
- education
- health concerns

These things can create:

- anxiety
- frustration
- confusion
- overwhelm
- guilt
- shame
- regret
- anger
- and more.

These emotions can cause feelings of unhappiness, misery, or being stuck in a rut and can lead to depression, despair, or even self-destruction.

The struggles of life can be so real that we can't even imagine anything better. When we are feeling down, it's almost impossible to see the greater possibilities that exist all around us.

At the deepest, hardest parts of life, when life gets heavy enough, one might say they are "low in spirit". A way out of the struggle is hard to see. The spirit is unclear.

Here's a metaphor I like to use to explain this.

Have you ever seen one of those Magic Eye stereogram illusion pictures?

At first, it just looks like a mess of nothing but jumbled colors. (maybe like your life?)

But then you follow the directions and refocus your eyes in just the right way, aaaand... Voila!

Now you can see the dolphin or spaceship in 3D!?! (maybe like the possibilities of your life?)

Think about it... The dolphin or spaceship was always there, you just weren't looking at it the right way, right?

You're also looking at your life in one way and may be convinced that's just the way it is. What I'm presenting to you is another way to see your life and the wonderful possibilities that are around you at this very moment.

What's more, this book will give you the instructions on how to "see" in a new way.

"Clarity of the human spirit" is achieved when one has been able to let go of and release the "struggles of the spirit" and they are no longer stuck in their "stuff".

By "struggles", I am referring to the emotions, beliefs and attitudes that block and blind one to the greater possibilities around them. Many call all that stuff, "emotional baggage". We all have our share, know what I mean?

But once those emotions and beliefs have been eliminated, there is a clarity of spirit that reveals a new and wonderful way of seeing life and living it.

This new "identity", *your* new "identity", moves forward in life with a confidence and peace that can be felt deep in the soul. It's a change in the "felt sense" of who you are. You live closer to your truth.

The changes you'll be able to make will often be quite palpable. What amazes people is how this "Magical State of Being", will affect and organize their life before they even get there or "arrive".

You think finding the perfect parking spot is Magic? Wait 'til you start to see the real Magic of the human spirit!

Authentic Magic And The Core Method... A Reality Check

Now, is it possible for *you* to become this person... this Authentic Magician?

Yes, it is.

Will it happen overnight?

No, it won't.

Why not?

Because, as I tell people I work with... it's like me teaching someone how to play chess for the first time. It's really a pretty simple game and I can have the new person playing with me in five or ten minutes.

But getting good at the game takes time and experience.

Because so many people are just not willing or interested in taking the time to get good at the game, they never do.

But, in this case, we're talking about the game of life... your life. So I'm going out on a limb and make the assumption this is important to you. That's why you're reading this book.

Your subconscious mind holds all of your habits, old and new and it doesn't tend to change them easily. Lucky for you the method works on habits too. Once you understand The Core Method and how to apply it, you will have the ability to even change old habits.

In fact, as you start using the method, you will begin to notice changes in your life from the beginning. Little ones here and there that will add up quickly to changing you enough that people will wonder what you're doing. I've seen it many times.

This is because I always encourage people to start clearing their greatest problems in life first. Clearing the big ones first will generally give you the most noticeable changes up front with the method. This can be very encouraging.

Start using The Core Method to let go of all that blocks your happiness, your peace and your love. Do this as often as possible. Do it every day. And as you do, you will begin to change who you are... your "identity".

This, in turn, will change your relationship with your world. As a result, it won't be long before you begin to live your own life of Authentic Magic in a world of your own choosing. Your fate is truly in your hands no matter what life seems to be handing you.

BTW, that last line is VERY important... "no matter what life seems to be handing you".

This means... "regardless of circumstances".

Ponder that idea. Do not take that concept lightly. I mean, how do you stop a person who has no resistance or need to push, force or fight?

What can stand in the way of someone who flows around all obstacles like water and lives in peace?

For this person, the good stuff of life flows into their life "with ease". They simply allow it all to come in and take its place.

This is why the Authentic Magician does not look out into the world and decide what's possible based on what they see.

No, the Authentic Magician looks into their heart and soul and decides "who they are" deep inside. They can then choose the elements of life that fit best and live it. This is not a fantasy. It's a promise. So, if you're ready to change your "identity" and your life...

Let Us Begin

Part One

1

Identity...
Who Are You, Really?

Wanna have a great time for the rest of your life? Here's what you do…

Drop all your fear of being judged. Let go of your fear of rejection. Release every insecurity. Let go of shame, guilt, hatred and all your anxiety.

Release self-consciousness, jealousy, remorse, sadness and regret. None of these help you anyway. Also let go of limiting beliefs, and negative judgments. Let all that fall away and live the rest of your life without any of it.

Wouldn't you have more fun that way? Yaaaay!
Sound like a plan? Surrrrre!

And you probably think I'm crazy, right? Easier said than done, right?

Maybe. Maybe not. OK, let's start small and work up.

Think of the one thing, the biggest thing you deal with every day that you feel is the hardest for you. Start with the one thing that seems to cause the greatest pain, discomfort or sorrow in your life.

Maybe it's:
- Anxiety? People judging you?
- Fear of failing at something really important?
- A relationship falling apart?

- Wishing you *knew* what you wanted in life?
- People you can't seem to get along with?
- Loss of a loved one?
- A health problem?
- Hating your job or boss?
- Lack of money and creditors hounding you?
- Wishing you were "there" instead of "here"?
- Impatience for something to happen?
- Lamenting a particular mistake?

Whatever it is, think of it.

Now, do the best you can to imagine what your life would be like if you removed this one pain from your life. Just let yourself imagine how you would feel once that one thing is gone and you know you never have to deal with it again.

Imagine a place or a time or a situation you could be in that would show you how wonderful your life is now that that one thing is gone and no longer hurts or bothers you.

Can you do that?

Because if you can, you have a small idea of what The Core Method can do for you.

And believe me, I know this can seem a bit far fetched, or hard to believe, but please stay with me. Once you have learned how the method works and have used it for a short time, I believe you will be pleasantly surprised.

2

The Invisible Secret of Life

Want to know this little secret? Here it is...

You don't get what you "want" in life.
You get "who you are".
This is why "identity" is so important.

In other words, you don't necessarily get the life you dream of or struggle for because *you may not be a match to what you want.* Instead, you will tend to get a life that matches *who you are...* your "identity". Who you are "being".

This is why people often joke that, "Life is what happens to you while you're busy making other plans."

For many people, who they are being is likely not a match to their dreams and this can be very frustrating. Why? Because they don't see the connection!

You see, your "identity" is made up of much more than what you look like or what's on your ID card.

*Your "identity" is a **trick of the mind!***

It's actually made up of a combination of things that exist as "energy" patterns in your mind. The effects of these energy patterns are stored in your body. And this is the energy that you are putting out to the world. And remember... energy attracts.

In your mind, these are things like your values, your beliefs, your attitudes, your opinions and your judgments. In your body, these are the energies of your emotions.

Together, these make up who you are "being" at this very moment. If you change any one of these, you have made a change in who you are being... your "identity". This will have an effect on how you feel about yourself and how you relate to and experience your world.

Another aspect of "identity" is what we associate with. Often people gradually develop tendencies to "identify" with all kinds of things in life.

Causes, styles, politics, hobbies, religions, conflict, peace, music, food, exercise... you name it and there are people who identify with it. Social groups and clubs are built around these things.

There are also many who identify with failure in life. It's a part of their "identity".

Ever hear this old adage... "If it weren't for bad luck, I'd have no luck at all"? Or how about this one... "I'm so broke, I can't even pay attention". Yes, there are people who actually believe things like these and their life seems to constantly prove it.

Believe it or not, the same goes for pain and suffering. People actually identify with pain and suffering to the point where they wouldn't know who they are without their pain and suffering.

Do you know anyone like that? Maybe intimately?

What's more, it's quite often true that others who know that person also recognize them as "one who suffers".

Recognize? Yes. It's an "identity". Identity is an inside job. We make it up.

No one forces you to be who you are "being". You just "do you", right? Well, who are you?

Have you always been the way you are now? Are you happy with all that? Or are there some things about you and your life you wish you could change? Most people have a list of things.

The question this book puts to you is… What if it was possible?

Look at your life and keep that last question in your mind as you read on.

3

A Reality Check About Your Choices

This may be hard to hear but it's a serious reality of your life.

Your "identity" is determining the quality of your life and future at this very moment. Are you OK with where it's taking you?

What I mean is, when people don't look within and resolve their inner conflicts and clear their path in life, or clear their spirit, they end up settling for living life with their default "identity", living the excuse... "This is just who I am!"

This too often means they end up settling for a life of mediocrity or less. And people who do this risk losing everything.

But I also want you to know this... there's more to you than meets the eye.

Your physical appearance can be recognized easily and the assumption will be that this is you. But your actual "identity" in this world is not physical, it's a trick of the mind. Stage hypnosis can easily prove this.

Ever see a stage hypnosis show? Those people suddenly believe things that make them act in ways that would totally baffle their closest family and friends... if it were not a hypnosis show. This is what I mean when I say "identity" is a trick of the mind.

In reality, it's the combination of the several elements of your psychology mentioned before. Remember? Your values, beliefs, attitudes, opinions and judgements, etc? These are what determines the kind and quality of the choices and decisions you make about who you are.

The choices and decisions your "identity" makes results in the kind and quality of the life you live. So when it comes time to make those big dreams come true, it will be a good idea to make sure you are the kind of person that matches those dreams. Because the law is...

"Like Attracts Like"

4

You Have Everything You Need to Make Huge Changes to Your Life

So how do people change their lives for the better?

Believe it or not, people change their lives by changing some part of their "identity". That's how you can see things differently. Therapists try to help people with this every day. Not always successfully.

Think about it...

Your experience of your life as it is now is the result of who you are at this moment.

And yes, I'm very aware that there are things that sometimes happen to us that we don't believe we have chosen or have anything to do with.

I counter this with the fact that there are things buried within all of us that we are not aware of.

We aren't aware of beliefs and emotions that have accumulated over time that affect our lives in mysterious and unknown ways. The energies of these beliefs and emotions affect our relationships, work, health, prosperity, feelings of safety and so much more.

These energies have everything to do with how your life goes.

When you make changes to your "identity", you're no longer the same person. This means you change the energies you carry and express into your world. And if that happens, how can you continue to live the same life?

You can't!

Know, this... every aspect of your beliefs, values, attitudes, opinions and judgments are susceptible to change.

Why?

Because all of these elements of your "identity" exist as energy patterns held in your subconscious mind. Where everyday life is concerned, these energy patterns can be changed by new information, different decisions, big events and life changing experiences.

Changing these aspects of your "identity" will change your emotional states or how you "feel" about yourself. As a result, your life and your experience of your world will always follow who you are "being" in order to match.

The energies of your "identity" can change as easily as this...

You may "believe" the neighborhood you live in is safe... until you come home one evening and discover your house has been broken into and you've been robbed. (From feeling safe to unsafe in a moment of shock and disbelief? Living life a little more wary of your surroundings?)

You may put a high "value" in a company's products... until they cut back and cheapen them with shoddy materials. (Feeling cheated with a simple realization? Not so trusting anymore?)

Your state of mind or "attitude" might be quite pleasant one morning on your way to work... until that jerk cuts you off and makes you slam on the brakes. (Feeling angry in an instant? Colors your mood for the rest of your day?)

Your "opinion" of your cool new next door neighbors might change one Tuesday night at 2 AM during their loud and annoying party.

(Feeling disrespected? Doubting your judgement of character now?)

And your "judgment" of that new neighbor might change again when he puts your garbage cans out to the curb just in time the next morning because he's still up... and you forgot! (Feeling sheepish? A little guilty?)

Yeah, "who" you are "being" can change in an instant. But it doesn't have to be because of the craziness of life. You can do it on purpose when you have a plan for your life. Read on.

5

Changing the Elements of Your Identity

What if your "values" in life changed?

Do you value adventure in life, or do you value a more sedate and peaceful existence?

Do you value integrity and dignity, or do you not mind living on the edge and bending the rules now and then?

Do you value peace at any cost or are you comfortable with confrontation?

Change any one of your values and you'll find your life automatically leading you into new experiences that match your new values. Google "a list of values" and take stock of yours.

You might find you have values that are keeping you from living the life you've dreamed of. You might not know until you look.

What if what you "believe" about yourself and the world changed?

Do you believe in yourself and your abilities or are you a little insecure and unwilling to take a chance in life? Does it bother you if there's too much attention put on you?

Do you believe the world is out to get you or do you believe you are safe in your world?

Do you enjoy working with other people or are you more comfortable working alone?

Our beliefs set us up for the very things that we experience. The tricky part is that we don't necessarily know all the deep seated beliefs we may have.

Things happen to us and we often don't make the connection to that part of us... that belief that pulled it in.

Do certain patterns seem to keep repeating in your life?

What belief would you have to have in order for that "thing" to keep happening to you over and over?

What if your "attitude" toward people and events changed?

Do you take a little kidding with a sense of humor or do you tend to get upset if people have a little fun at your expense?

Do you tend to see the advantages in situations or do you tend to get frustrated at the problems life deals out?

Do you tend to feel humbled at praise or do you strut around and act like you deserve the glory?

Your attitude has much to do with how others experience you. Have you ever had a change of attitude about some conflict and noticed how others attitudes change as well?

A simple change of attitude can change your world. Remember this if you ever get pulled over by a cop. Your attitude can have much to do with the outcome.

What if your "opinions" about people and things changed?

What is your opinion of people who cheat?

What is your opinion of religion?

What is your opinion of your boss?

How do you feel about the place you're living in?

How do you view people with less education than yours?

What about people who live a different lifestyle than yours?

The possibilities are endless. The thing is, carrying negative opinions about anything charges your inner being with destructive energies. The serious problem with this is that these energies tend to eat at you from the inside.

It's that old line about drinking poison hoping the other person will die. Negative opinions are the seeds of disease. Letting go of these kinds of opinions could prolong your life and make living it more enjoyable.

What if your "judgments" about people, events and yourself... changed?

Do you know the effects of judging someone harshly? Has that ever happened to you?

If someone you have a low opinion of succeeds, how do you feel about that?

Do you tend to level negative judgments against yourself if you fail or do you give yourself room to fail so you can try again with new hope?

Know anyone you feel needs to pay for their wrongdoings? Do you hope karma will get them? Is there a judgment in there somewhere?

Enough focus on negative judgments can often pull into your life the very things you wish on others. It isn't necessary to suddenly approve of those you hold negative judgments about. It's actually best to *become neutral about them.*

No hate. Just peace. Later, I will share my three rules about that. In the meantime, allow them to be. They will attract their own karma, a subject I will cover later in this book.

From a place of inner peace, you can accomplish much to affect your world and those you may "disagree" with. At least your experience of them will cause you less stress which is healthy. And healthy is good.

These are simple examples of how little parts of your psychology or "identity" can change because of simple decisions, events and experiences you might have.

Things like these examples above can make little tweaks in your "identity" or who you "thought you were". (Past tense?)

These little tweaks may change the kind and quality of the choices and decisions you make and things you do, and these new choices, decisions and actions are going to affect the kind and quality of the life you live.

After all, we always try to make the best choices and decisions for ourselves and those we care about. Those choices and decisions come from who we are... our "identity".

If simple decisions, events and experiences like these can change how we feel, how we act, what we believe and ultimately what we do and experience as life, then apparently we have some kind of access to who we are, our "identity", and we might be able to choose the changes we make.

Having access to that kind of control is what this book is about.

6

The Incredible Impact of Your Emotions

There's one more very important element of your "identity".

Yes, it's true, we all have our beliefs, values, attitudes, opinions and judgments. These result in our choices, decisions, actions and life experiences.

But there's one more part of us that actually has one of the greatest effects on the quality of our lives... our "emotions".

Most people have no clue about all that deep stuff that lies buried in our psyches, but we all *feel* our emotions because they tend to come right to the surface and grab our attention whether we like it or not. In fact, our emotions seem to be the thing we deal with the most in our lives.

> **Your emotional state is rooted in your "identity" and in any given situation it's going to be the final determining factor in the kind and quality of the life you live.**

If your emotional state is shot, life sucks. On the other hand, if your emotional state is strong, you shine like a star!

7

The Significance of These Kinds of Changes

Remember that list of things I pointed out where the changes came from experiences and such? Your values, beliefs, attitudes, opinions and judgments? Consider the people who know you. Will they all still feel the same about you if you change these things about yourself in significant ways?

Of course, the changes would be favorable to you. People are attracted to change if they know their life will improve with a little Magic. It's natural to want the best for ourselves and those we care about.

What if you became less impatient? Less afraid? Less ashamed, guilt ridden, anxious or angry?

What if you were able to ease your own stress? Make yourself lighter and happier? Put a light in your eyes that wasn't there before? People notice things like that. They may even ask how you're doing it.

Would it be okay to feel good about yourself? Even "love" yourself? Does that thought make you uncomfortable? It does for many. A lot of people carry a lot of guilt and shame or worse. What if all that disappeared? Would you be OK with that?

What if these changes made you easier to get along with? More patient? More fun? More courageous, capable and creative? Even more excited for your future?

What if you discovered a way to make yourself richer? More free? What if you made changes that improved your lifestyle?

What if you became unafraid to be vulnerable? More willing to listen? To care? To love others?

Would the people who knew you before still recognize you the same way? Would you recognize the old you anymore?

Would you want to?

What if you could make the kind of changes that caused you to become more intuitive, open and willing in life?

What if making these changes allowed experiences, things and people into your life that improved it in wonderful ways? What if they created in you an inner knowing that you will always be able to handle and even enjoy whatever comes your way, even if it's challenging?

In fact, what if these changes made you more "attractive"? Not just better looking, (which does happen on occasion) but magnetic to the things, experiences and people you choose for yourself and your life?

If you're not the same person you were, how could you live the same old life?

Know this...

Changes in your values, beliefs, attitudes, opinions and judgments about yourself and life can and will cause changes in your mental and emotional states, which are actual changes in your "identity"... *who you are.*

This will lead to better relationships, better health and will also improve the quality of the life you live.

You've likely dreamed of and wished for certain things in your life to be different. Better. Changing your "identity" is how it's done. This is the reality of what I'm talking about.

8

The Power of Authentic Magic
This is The Core Method

What is Authentic Magic?

It's a reality you were born with. An ability few have come to understand and apply effectively or with intention.

Many experience their default mental and emotional settings and complain about their lives. Some make their Magic work spectacularly and live amazing lives.

It's a choice we all have.

Authentic Magic is what happens when you clear your "baggage" out of the way so your spirit can spread out, touch the Universe and make things happen for you. Happy accidents, positive chance encounters and lucky breaks.

It's like your own personal universal valet charged with taking care of things and making sure your path is clear. It prepares your way in life by making the necessary arrangements so your plans go more to your liking. This is the result of living in the "Magical State". (I'll describe this state later)

Your state of being, this Magical State, adjusts and sets a tone for your life which determines your frequency. This is done by applying The Core Method. The Core Method simply makes use of natural born parts of you. And all of this will be explained in detail soon.

Part Two

9

Creating a Foundation

I just introduced you to the concept of Authentic Magic which describes the effects of using The Core Method. In this part, I am going to introduce you to several other concepts that will set the foundation for your use of The Core Method.

Of all of the healing methods I learned and experienced, I resonated the most with those that fall into the category of "Energetic Psychology". This is because everything that makes up our psychology is stored in us in the form of energy.

You can look up any or all of the healing methods I refer to online, there's a reference list in the back of the book too. These are the methods by which I was able to bring about the most profound changes in myself and others.

From my stories in the introduction, my first exposure was to TFT. (Thought Field Therapy) Remember where I discovered Voodoo? Once I got into TFT, I soon discovered EFT. (Emotional Freedom Techniques).

Both of these methods are related as EFT is a simplified form of TFT. And they both require one to physically "tap" on specific points of the body that directly affect the corresponding acupressure meridians found there. This tapping causes an adjustment to the emotion being focused on based on one's "intention". In this work, intention is "king". You'll see this as I go along.

A meridian in the body is like a brook in a forest. It flows into a creek which flows into a stream which flows into a river, etc. In a river, the flow is water. In a meridian of the body, the flow is energy. Like brooks, creeks, streams and rivers, meridians also connect up to one main river.

The "main river" in the body is called the Governing Meridian in Chinese acupuncture. It starts at the upper lip, runs up the forehead, over the head, down the back of the neck and down the spine to the tailbone.

The smaller meridian of this system goes from the tailbone up the front of the body to the chin.

All other meridians branch out from these two.

The Chinese have known about these energy flows in the body for thousands of years. It took me several years, but I finally came to realize that there's something very special about the Governing Meridian. Stay with me. You'll see what I mean.

The next method I discovered was Dr. Brad Mays ECC (Emotional Complex Clearing) The actual clearing modality in ECC is a combination of taking one through a guided visualization... and stroking down the spine (the Governing Meridian) several times with the fingertips.

But because I couldn't do this stroking thing down my own spine very well, I tended to stick to the EFT tapping because I could reach all the points and tap on them.

Let me tell you, ECC is extremely powerful and changes lives in one very short session. I know this because Dr. May did it with me. However, this experience was early in my Energetic Psychology education, so I didn't get the connection between EFT and ECC then. That would come later.

ECC is also where I learned "Muscle Testing" which became a permanent part of my work. It's a quick way to talk to the subconscious mind and find out what's going on in there.

Later when I learned about the Emotion Code from Dr. Brad Nelson, I realized he also uses muscle testing in all of his work. Again, this is because it's the quickest and most effective way to discover the secrets hidden deep down in your own psyche.

I *highly* recommend you go to YouTube and search it. Learning how to communicate with your own subconscious is one of the most valuable things you can do.

It's part of the focusing work you can do to discover what's blocking your Magic. Once you know what it is, you'll have the method to release it and be free of it.

From my own perspective, muscle testing is a very important part of inner work. You'll see this more as I get into The Core Method.

10

The Plot Thickens

Many years later, I discovered Dr. Brad Nelson's Emotion Code. Here again, the actual healing was done by stroking down the spine (the Governing Meridian) with the fingertips.

From all I know about ECC and the Emotion Code, the two men who created these methods do not know each other. They both got this technique from some other source I'm not aware of. Again, the Emotion Code is extremely powerful. Amazing healing can be accomplished in one very short session.

At this point, I had learned:
- EFT - which taps on meridian points that all connect up to the Governing Meridian.
- ECC - which calls for stroking down the middle of the back or spine or the Governing Meridian with the fingertips.
- The Emotion Code - which also requires one to stroke down the Governing Meridian with the fingertips.

Obviously, I am bringing your attention to the fact that all three of these very powerful healing methods have this one thing in common... the spine or Governing Meridian.

Back then, I was still very into EFT. So I didn't see the connection yet. But hang on. It's coming.

Then I discovered a few extra tools I didn't know I needed that became quite valuable.

A couple of years after I learned the Emotion Code, I discovered and learned both The Release Technique and The Sedona Method.

Both of these methods are related because they both came from one man, Lester Levenson who lived in the mid 20th century.

The Release Technique takes a different tack to healing and is a bit more complicated than The Sedona Method but both are very effective in their own way. Neither of them utilizes the Governing Meridian but they both shared some concepts that I found to be very effective and useful as I began to see the correlations later on between all I was learning.

You'll learn those concepts too when I take you through The Core Method. I'm just letting you know that some of The Core Method came from these two modalities. I'll explain them soon.

By that point, I was deep into Energetic Psychology. I was learning more and more about the human condition and how people work inside energetically. What's more, I was excited and humbled by how I could help people with what I knew.

But what came next really expanded my mind.

11

Two Main Elements of The Core Method

Your Awareness is an Element of The Core Method

Have you ever noticed how once you get interested in something, it seems to be everywhere? Like, you buy a certain kind or color of car and suddenly you notice them every time you turn around?

Yeah, me too. With the focus I had on the amazing healing techniques I had been discovering, I was soon exposed to several new and amazing things that radically changed how I worked with myself and other people.

My next adventure in Energetic Psychology came from Jason Mangrums book, "Uberman - Almost Superhuman". In the second chapter, it talked about a centering exercise. Not long after that, this led me to Paul Wong and his "Art Of Neutrality" because they are very similar.

The amazing thing about this modality is that it made use of the center or midline of the body... but there was no tapping or stroking. In fact, nothing physical at all. It was all done with the mind by directing one's "awareness".

This was exactly what I was looking for all these years. A way to do the same work "covertly" all on the inside where no one would know. It also only took about two or three seconds to run through it. Much quicker than tapping meridians points or stroking down the spine with the fingers.

With this modality, I came to realize that awareness is not just something we do. Awareness is a "thing". You can place it on something or someone and it will affect what you place it on.

Example: Have you ever been out somewhere, maybe just relaxing and having a cup of coffee and suddenly you get the feeling someone is watching you? So you casually turn and just happen to look the person right in the eyes?

Yeah. That person put their awareness on you and you felt it. Weird, huh?

This is a pretty common experience. The reason you feel it is because awareness affects what you place it on. People who go into an old house sometimes get the feeling there is someone else there and they are being watched.

There are many TV shows about haunted houses, hotels and forests where people get that feeling.

Generally this is because there are spirits (or maybe even other people) watching the individual. Maybe you've felt this in some old house or strange place. Or maybe just sitting out in public somewhere.

Try this: Hold out your hand palm up and gently "place" your awareness in your palm. Leave it there for several seconds. Just be really aware of the palm of your hand. Notice what happens.

You might notice your palm will begin to feel different. A warmth or tingling can occur. Put your awareness on one of your feet for several seconds. It will do the same thing.

If you put your awareness on someone who is intensely focused on something, as in, they are mentally busy, they may not notice your awareness because the effects of awareness are a subtle thing.

But if they are relaxed, watch them and see what happens. It can be spooky... or annoying. Just be careful. You might get caught staring.

When I realized this awareness thing, I remembered stories I had heard from several people from back in my EFT days.

A practitioner got on a plane for a trip. As they waited for the plane to taxi to the strip and take off, they noticed someone across the aisle who was fidgeting and acting nervous.

They realized the nervous person was likely afraid of flying. So the EFT practitioner did this "mental" thing and started covertly tapping on themselves for the nervous one. In other words, they did it all mentally.

Son of a gun... it worked!

The practitioner saw a noticeable difference in the nervous person as they seemed to calm down and settle in for the flight.

I also remembered that in the Emotion Code, the practitioner could do the same "thing". It's called "proxy" work. They could put their awareness on the other person and do the work for them.

About this time I also discovered Elma Mayer and her "Now Healing" which just happened to work basically the same way the Art Of Neutrality did.

Then I discovered why.

The Art Of Neutrality, Now Healing, and I'm thinking Jason's book, Uberman, all came from Kam Yuen, a 35th generation Shaolin Master. He was one of the technical advisors for the fight scenes in the TV show, Kung Fu. He was also an extra in the show.

The story I heard was that long ago, he and his master both got together and decided it was time to bring this one Shaolin technique out to the public. Now I don't know for sure this is exactly how it happened. But ultimately, Kam is responsible for this work. He calls his technique the Yuen Method.

Your Center or Mid-line is an element of The Core Method

So, how do these methods I learned work?

They all rely on the concept of placing one's awareness into the midline or center of the body in a specific way.

In The Core Method, I take it just a bit further and say put your awareness back deep inside, back to the spine or to your Governing Meridian.

Remember on the back of this book I say, "In the middle of your life is the Access Point to change your life?" Where is the center of your life? It's in the middle of your head. It's your awareness.

Your entire life is experienced through your awareness. Where is the access point to change your life? It's in the middle of your body. Your midline or the "core" of your body.

The governing meridian is extremely sensitive to not only your awareness, but also to your "intention" because the subconscious mind is part of the equation and knows what you intend. After all, the subconscious mind is energy too!

With The Core Method, you put your awareness into your center (or midline) with a specific intention. Doing so causes a change (or release) in what is intended.

You're working with a very sensitive energetic system in your body that, believe it or not, is intimately connected to all that makes up your "identity".

All that stuff deep inside of you… your values, beliefs, attitude, opinions and judgments. All of your internal organs and even your habits.

But most importantly? Your emotions. This will all be explained when I take you through The Core Method process. You'll get to try it in real time.

12

The Four Systems of the Core Which Make The Core Method Possible

As I worked with this new way to release old emotions and make changes in myself and other people, I began to ponder what was really going on. I wondered what all was involved with the Core of the body. Part of my research directed me to Greg Braden (look him up) and his exploration of...

the heart field.

It extends out from the heart or the center of the body by up to several feet and has one of the most profound effects on our emotional states and even our health.

In fact, it has been discovered that the heart actually has its own collection of neurons. These are brain cells. Yes, the heart "thinks"!

It does it's best to communicate its thoughts to the brain but does this through feelings. A thought within this heart field affects every level of your being. This is one of the reasons you "feel" things like someone's awareness being placed on you.

As I dug deeper into the Core, I realized another element...

the central nervous system.

It runs down through the spine and branches out just like those brooks, creeks, streams and rivers. Every single nerve and fiber of the body is touched by and connected to the central nervous system and is extremely sensitive to the slightest touch.

I believe it's sensitive to every thought too.

The central nervous system touches every single organ of the body. What's more, your subconscious mind is fully aware of the function of every single cell, chemical process, organ function, muscle function, thought and heartbeat of your body and the central nervous system is part of that. Nothing gets by the central nervous system.

Add to this...

the chakra system,

and its effect on our emotional states. It connects directly into the spinal column.

I looked this up to give you a quick idea of its effects on us. Here's what it said...

"The Chakras are responsible for radiating life energy, or prana. According to the Vedas, chakras have a direct influence on your ambitions and goals within a relationship. A blocked and disrupted chakra signals the onset of mental and spiritual health problems."

I will add that healthy chakras are tuned into your experience of your inner and outer worlds.

So you got that going for you.

The forth system?

The Governing Meridian.

Remember that one? Yeah, it's BIG!

Four extremely sensitive systems:
- The heart field
- The central nervous system
- The chakra system
- The governing meridian

All four of these systems are found in the center or core of your body and play their part in the process of the change work of The Core Method.

It's almost like all these elements around and in your spinal column are this highly sensitive antenna that receives communication from your awareness and environment to help you survive and thrive through the communication that goes on at all times.

I'd have to say now you know why you get "that feeling" when you're sitting out somewhere relaxing and having a cup of coffee.

Someone *is* watching you and your inner antenna or "core" feels it!

The human body is designed to sense all this. It really is a masterpiece of creation. And you've got one. Pretty neat, eh?

One Last Verification Before We Go On

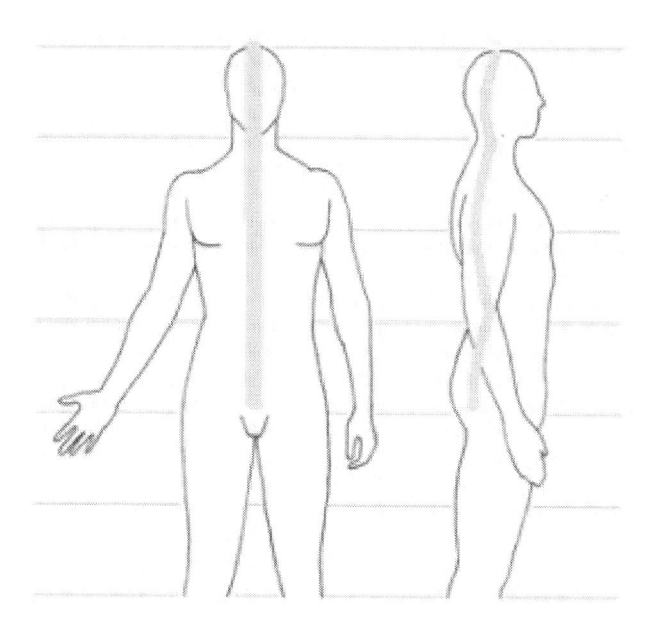

At this point, I will add one more source of information about the core of the body.

Several years ago, a Russian physicist by the name of Vadim Zeland wrote a book called Reality Transurfing. I think you might call it a philosophy of life and an amazing way to look at reality.

I highly recommend it. Just know that his book is well over 700 pages and runs about $40. I was already well into my own method as I read, so I looked at it from that standpoint.

Many things stood out to me as very powerful. But one thing in his book *really* stood out because of how I look at change work from an energetic point of view.

Vadim is a physicist of several years mind you. Quite scientific.

In the beginning of his chapter entitled, "Energy", he point-blank says that energy runs through the body in two directions. He says one current runs upward one inch in front of the spine in men and two inches in front of the spine in women.

Then he says the second current runs downward very close to the spine. More evidence that there is a heck of a lot going on with the center or "core" of the body. Especially right at the spine.

All of it is very sensitive and very connected to every part of our lives, the world we live in and to the Universe.

All it takes is a clear intention placed in the core in just the right way and things change and always for the better.

Part Three

13

Specific Core Method Elements

Your Subconscious Mind Runs About 90% of Your Life!

It's TRUE! All of your values, beliefs, attitudes, opinions and judgments are stored in your subconscious mind along with all of your memories and your habitual ways of being.

Every moment of your whole life is recorded and stored in your subconscious mind. This is because there's no limit to how much your subconscious mind can store. It's all just energy patterns!

Remember, memories and all that other stuff is nothing more than energy which has no dimensions and takes up no space. No matter how much knowledge and experience you gain, it all fits inside of your subconscious mind. Pretty amazing how all that stuff can affect us the way it does, right?

But that's not the case with your conscious mind. Experts say the conscious mind can only process seven - plus or minus two - bits of information at a time. There's no way your conscious mind could hold all the "stuff" of your life . You'd go nuts in minutes.

Your whole life is stored below your conscious awareness, so there are things about you that get buried and forgotten.

That is, until the moment you experience something that brings up an old memory, belief, attitude or opinion, etc. The problem is, too often when old forgotten stuff comes up, it causes chaos we aren't prepared for or ready to deal with.

This means your subconscious mind is not only holding all you need to succeed in life like your knowledge, talents, abilities and skills, it's also holding all it would take to destroy your life like your bad habits, negative attitudes, fears and other baggage.

Your subconscious mind is like a child. If you ignore it, it will likely get you into mischief and too often does. This is because it doesn't know the difference between right or wrong, good or bad.

I REPEAT – it doesn't know the difference between right or wrong, good or bad!

You must guide it and consciously choose what you want it to do or it will create havoc in your life. It simply doesn't choose what you put into it or what you will have in your life.

You must consciously choose that for yourself and tell your subconscious to make it so. Yes, you can actually do that.

Here's another layer for you...

Human beings are creatures of habit!

- Your subconscious mind maintains all of your *habits*.
- Your subconscious mind is running your habits *right now*.
- It's *very* easy to fall back into bad habits.
- Habits, good or bad, are *comfortable*.
- Habits are comfortable because they are *familiar*.
- Some habits may be destroying your happiness and success.

Your subconscious mind also holds all of your memories, your personality, your self image, your hopes and your dreams.

It also holds the reasons for all of your small thinking and your fears including all of the reasons your hopes and dreams may never come true.

The emotions we have felt about events in our lives are stored in the subconscious. What's more, they are like individual engines that are running 24 hours a day, 365 days a year just waiting for the right thing to happen to bring them to the surface.

You might be familiar with this scenario. You're driving along, happy as a lark and doing just fine until... *that one song comes on the radio.*

You know the one. It takes you right back to that time and place, with that person or those people... and the tears start to flow.

Your emotions about that time and place are triggered by that familiar song. Emotions you may have thought were handled and in the past and forgotten. Oh, no no no. It's all there just waiting for the chance to get your attention. And for a reason I will tell you soon.

The good news is you have access to all of that... and you can change it.

When you aren't aware of what's hidden in your subconscious, it will run your life because it's all a part of your "identity".

Becoming aware of that "stuff" makes it possible to change your "identity" and your life.

"Until you make the unconscious conscious, it will run your life and you will call it fate". Carl Jung.

14

The Emotion Connection

I hope you will be patient with me. I know I am repeating myself about a lot of things here. But it's so important for you to get what I'm saying.

It's said that repetition is the mother of learning. How many self-help books have you read and then just set on the shelf and forgotten? Even I have been guilty of this.

What if you had taken just half of what you've read seriously and applied it. Is it possible that if you had, you'd be living on easy street by now? Think about it.

Let's go on.

Every Thought Generates a Feeling or Emotion

But only... *Every. Single. One.*

It might be a "positive" thought or a "negative" thought. It might even be a "neutral" thought. But if you'll notice, as you think it, there's a feeling or emotional state in your body that goes with it.

Think of the last great time you had. Something you did with friends, family or with that one special person. Or maybe it was some great accomplishment.

Once you have thought of that experience, notice how you feel in your body when you hold that memory. And notice that the thought is in your mind... and the feeling is in your body.

Now, think of something that happened that got you upset. A breakup with a significant other. A breakdown on the road. A trip to the hospital. Someone you love getting hurt.

Again, notice the thought is in your mind and the feeling is in your body. These are the two parts of any experience. The head part and the body part.

Your emotional state changes with every thought, even if the changes are gentle and subtle... almost unnoticeable. From wistful daydreaming to replaying the last fight you had over and over in your mind, when you "think" about any part of your life, you "feel" it.

But even more, ANY time something happens that bothers you, any problem you experience, from a problem at work or at home to any sad old memory popping up, notice the emotion. Notice it! Pay attention to it because it's letting you know it's there. And for a good reason!

The reason these emotions come up is partly because feeling emotions is a natural response to life. The other part is because by your emotions coming up and you being aware of this, you get to have a choice!

Yes! Your emotions are giving you a choice! Do you like the emotion? Do you like how you feel... or not? Are you OK with how you feel? Or do you wish you didn't feel that way? It's important for you to start becoming aware this way.

Why?

Because The Core Method removes or deletes the negative emotions, and it does this in seconds. It removes the blocks to your Magic! And the more negative emotions you eliminate from your life, the more Magic you experience and the smoother your life will flow.

In other words, you don't "have" to feel sad, bad or worse anymore if you don't want to. You have a choice. You have The Core Method.

When negative emotions come up, now you can let them go!

Your Values, Beliefs, Attitudes, Opinions and Judgments are all Thoughts and They ALL Generate Emotions

This is why you will be able to release them if you wish!

Every single one of these elements of your "identity" are basically a story stored in your deeper mind. And every one of them manifest as the energy of emotion. You can use The Core Method to eliminate the effects of any of the elements of your "identity" that do not serve you.

Consider that the "human condition" is vast and complex. To simplify, one can say that your life is filled by the three main categories of experience... health, wealth and happiness.

How you experience the vast majority of these three is dependent on your mental and emotional states, or as I have called them, your "identity"... who you are.

What's more, a basic fact of your life is...

100% of what blocks your Magic is found in your "identity".

All of your relationship problems, your money problems and most of your health problems are rooted in your "identity" which is all energy.

I do realize that a broken leg is not just an energetic experience. It will take the expertise of a qualified doctor to reset the bones so they can heal. But the rest of your life is pretty much all about energy.

When you clear your emotional blocks, the Magic of your spirit will begin to flow through your life like water down a stream, unbothered by the boulders life may serve up.

Every Emotion Has a Specific Intensity

You can feel your emotions any time and gauge just how intense they are on a zero to ten scale. "zero" is, "no problem". "ten" is, "take me to the ER!" (just kidding, but emotions can get pretty intense)

When you're beginning to work with the method, it's good to keep track of your emotional intensity because this way, you can objectively measure your progress as you let go of the blocks.

Not only this, but your emotions also have a *location* in your body. And if you focus on them, you can generally point to where they are stuck.

This means you can measure the intensity of an emotion and locate where it is in your body. This will help eliminate the vagueness of your emotions and make them more of an object you can get your mental hands on. Your emotions and such cease to be this nebulous "thing" you don't know what to do with. Now you'll know what you're working with.

Most of the work you'll do will cause a noticeable "felt sense" of change. Measuring your progress with a problem on the "zero" to "ten" scale will be encouraging and make you want to use the method on the next thing in your life. In other words, it feels good to make noticeable progress. The Core Method does that.

Please know that you won't have to keep measuring as you get comfortable with the method. There will come a time soon when you'll just think the thought, feel the emotion, do the method in a few seconds and be on your way. It's really just that simple.

Months of therapy done in 2 minutes for free. Neat, huh?

15

Every Problem In Life Has Two Parts

The first part of every problem is the "story" or what happened. Or it might still be happening if it's not over.

But it's a "story".

The story is a "mind" thing which means we "think" about it. The story is stored in memory. It has a beginning, middle and end (if it's over).

You'll always be able to tell the "story". And boy, do we love to tell our stories!

Oh. My. Gosh!

We really get twisted up in our stories telling them over and over to ourselves and to anyone willing to listen. Wanna know why? Because we "identify" with our stories.

They are *us*! Relationship stories, health stories, work stories, money stories... you name it and someone has a story to tell.

The second part of every problem is the "emotion" our stories generate.

We tell the story or think about the story and feel the emotion. The emotion is a "body" thing so we feel it.

Funny thing about the emotion part though. We typically don't know what to do with that part. We know how to tell the story, and we do.

But the emotion is just so much nebulous energy churning around inside our bodies that no one ever told us what to do with. It's this "energy in motion" thing or some call it "E-Motion".

We can tell the "story" and get all kinds of love, empathy, sympathy or whatever from people. Remember, misery loves company? We're looking for some way to feel better. When we feel others are in our misery with us, we don't feel so alone in our suffering. I guess it helps... a little.

But the emotion?

We just feel it and wish we didn't and don't know what to do about it. Oh, we "cope" with our emotions as best as we can. We may eat more, go shopping, play video games, have more sex, drink more alcohol, take more drugs... whatever.

As long as we don't have to "feel" bad about our "stories".

But all these are just *coping*, which never works long term and it never resolves why we feel our emotions. All coping does is push those feelings back down inside so they can fester even more.

Believe it or not, most diseases of the body come from coping too long with negative emotions. You don't want to do that.

When A Problem Gets Broken

Think about this...

In order for a problem in your life to be fully functional, it must have both of these parts... the story and the emotion.

Example: So and so did X to you and now you're mad. That's a complete problem, right? You have a story, or what X did to you, and you have an emotion... anger.

You have something to talk about and you have the motivation to do so because the emotion drives you to want to talk about it. You want to tell everybody what so and so did! So you tell anyone who will listen. Except for us guys. We never do that. (HA!)

Now, let me ask you...

If either of these two parts is missing, do you still have a problem?

I mean, if you have no "story", what are you going to talk about?

Nothing. You're all good.

What if you have no emotion about a story?

You have no motivation to even care. Therefore, you have no problem. You're all good.

Either way, if one or the other is gone, no problem.

Broken problems equal no problems. And no problems equal Magic!

16

Your Two States – "Wanting" and "Having"

We human beings are incredibly complex creatures who exist in many different states all at the same time. Where The Core Method is concerned, these two states are vitally important for you to understand.

Believe it or not, you exist in these two states simultaneously at this very moment depending on what part of your life you address. The two states are "wanting" and "having".

Consider your life.

- Do you *have* a place to live? If you do, then you don't *want* a place to live... you *have* one.
- Do you *have* a car? If you do, then you don't *want* a car... you *have* one.
- Do you *have* a job? If you do, then you don't *want* a job... you *have* one.

Maybe you *have* these things but you want to upgrade them. You *want* the upgrades until you *have* them. Get the idea?

"Wanting" and "having" are a huge deal in our psychology. They touch every aspect of our life and establish our view of our world and how we interact with it. Of course there is a lot we don't care about either way. But those things are not important here. The only things important here are what you care about.

When you *want* something, you are without it. But when you *have* something, you own it. Two completely different states of being.

Let me point out one more aspect of these two states.

"Wanting" and "having" are like "ones" and "zeros" in computing. There's nothing in between or on either side. These are your only choices in life. It's like sitting and standing. You can only do one or the other.

If you're sitting, you're not standing. If you're standing, you're not sitting. You can't do both. You must choose.

The same goes for "wanting" and "having". In fact, they don't even know each other because they've never met! When one shows up, the other disappears! It's that literal!

"Wanting" and "having" are two sides of the same coin. Only one can be facing up at any given time.

I know this may seem rather simplistic just now, but I assure you, it will be one of the most profound elements of your life once you understand how The Core Method works.

Here's what I mean.

Do you *have* peace right now, or do you *want* it?
Do you *have* financial freedom right now, or do you *want* it?
Do you *have* good health right now, or do you *want* it?
Do you *have* a great relationship right now, or do you *want* one?

You see, "wanting" and "having" deeply affects your inner happiness. Let me go a little further and help you understand the power of these two states.

What is the Power of "Wanting"?
- Wanting is "lack".
- Wanting is not "having".
- Wanting is longing for.
- Wanting is emptiness, exclusion, incompleteness, hollowness, loneliness.
- Wanting is denial.
- Wanting admits something is missing.
- Wanting is the feeling of saying, "No" which can be a very empty feeling.

In fact, "wanting" is one of the most insidious problems in the world. In some cases, "wanting" is even akin to the experience of poverty. Like when people go without the basic necessities of life and want them. "Wanting" can even cause crime, violence and war.

Desire is "wanting" and "wanting" is not "having".

This means every time you express a desire to *have* something, or in other words, "want it", you are basically telling your deeper self that you don't *have* it. The feeling that "wanting" generates is one of lack, emptiness, or not "having".

Our deeper self is creative and can only work with what we give it, so what does our deeper self do with this "wanting" feeling?

It gives you more of the same... more "wanting". More "lack". It perpetuates the "wanting". Just think of something you've *wanted* for a long time. Thanks to your subconscious mind's ability to give you more of what you focus on, you still *want* that thing, right? How much longer are you going to go on "wanting" it?

This happens because your deeper self or subconscious mind does not know how to discriminate between what is "good" or "bad" for you.

This is also why people get into destructive frames of mind and bad habits. They don't realize their own subconscious mind will help them hurt and deprive themselves.

The deeper self gives you more of what you dwell on. That's one of its jobs. And that's what happens with desire or "wanting".

Sometimes I say to people, "What you dwell on - is what fills you up - is what shows up".

Some 2,500 years ago, Buddha said, "Desire is the cause of all suffering". He was right.

In fact, many people seem to hold the idea that denying themselves their dreams is somehow virtuous. That sacrifice is honorable... no matter what. They may even try to push these beliefs on others... like their children. This might be familiar to you. I don't know.

On the Other Hand, "Having" is the Answer!

What is the Power of "Having"?

"Having" is fulfillment, completeness, ownership, inclusion, abundance, peaceful, joyful and more.

"Having" is like saying, "Yes!" and "Yes" can be a very powerful feeling. In fact, for some people, it can even be overwhelming.

Interestingly, and maybe even sadly for a lot of people, "having" is forbidden. Too often we deny ourselves the pleasures we would truly love to have because we fear being seen as indulgent, extravagant, self gratifying, excessive, selfish or even sinful, etc.

Afraid of being judged?

These ideas may be buried deep in the psyche from childhood and as adults, we don't know it. This is why I say you *have* within your subconscious mind all you need to be happy and successful. But you may also *have* all that will bring misery, pain and failure.

Luckily, The Core Method can remove these darker ideas and set your inner tone to one of allowing the good stuff to come in.

Whether you actually have the new thing or situation or not is irrelevant. The *feeling* that you *have* it means everything to your deeper self. The feeling of "having" is the single most powerful response to "wanting".

There's a confidence and calmness in owning the assumption or feeling that what you've chosen now belongs to you. It's your emotions and feelings that your deeper self or subconscious mind responds to.

This is the basis of your Authentic Magic. As Neville Goddard says, "Feeling gets the blessing". He's right.

17

Why Negative Emotions Exist, What They Mean and How The Core Method Deals With Them

When you feel a negative emotion like anger, guilt, shame, anxiety, etc., you are experiencing a *lack* feeling.

This means something is missing. A "negative emotion" like anger, frustration, guilt, shame or whatever means there is something you are "wanting" but do not have. There is an emptiness or longing.

What is it you *want*?

There are three basic things in life we all *want* more than anything else. Three things that relate to all experiences, no matter what. When we don't have one or more of these three things, we feel an incomplete feeling.

A longing. A "wanting". An emptiness that cries for fulfillment.

A lacking feeling that nags at us until we obtain what's missing.

What Are The Three Things We All Want More Than Anything Else In Life?

They are...

Control – Approval – Safety

These three things affect everything in our lives... Our health, our wealth and our happiness.

When control, approval and safety are missing, we experience "wanting" them. How we know they are missing is when we are experiencing any negative emotion.

Fear, anger, jealousy, shame or whatever emotion it might be, all of them bring up "wanting" one or more of these three inner experiences.

Simple examples are...
- When things don't go the way we want, we *want* control.
- When people aren't friendly, we *want* approval.
- When we are afraid, we *want* safety.

Believe me when I say it can be a lot more complicated than this. I am only presenting the simple basics of this concept.

What's the answer to "wanting" control, approval or safety?

"Having" them!!!

As I have pointed out, you can only be in a state of "wanting" OR "having" at any one time. (Remember, they've never met?)

This means if you are "wanting" control, approval or safety and you release or let go of "wanting" them, you will automatically default into "having" control, approval and safety because it's the only other state available. Two options, "wanting" or "having".

The Goal Of The Core Method

The crux of The Core Method and Authentic Magic is to clear out the emotions to our stories so that we can think about them and feel nothing for them.

This does *not* mean you become numb to life. It means you have a choice. You can keep the emotion or let it go. With The Core Method, this is entirely up to you. If the story causes you to feel bad and you are ready to stop feeling bad, do the method.

When I helped the WWII veteran clear the emotion from his old story, suddenly, he could tell me what happened and not cry. It became easy for him to think about it and not feel bad anymore, which made it easy to talk about. He appreciated this very much! It released a heavy burden from his life!

Think about something in your life that makes you feel bad.

Past or present.

There's a story and an emotion and it's a block to your Magic.

What if you could think of it and it didn't bother you in the least? I mean, you know the story and you can tell the story. But when you do, it's like… "Meh, so what".

I did this work with one young lady for a couple of hours and then she continued on her own because the method is easy to do. She had been severely traumatized by a man and had serious PTSD from it.

By applying the method to all parts of her experience, she said now she could tell the story and it was no more bothersome than saying she went to the store for bread and milk.

That's when you become like water. No fighting. No resistance. No fuss. No hate. All you experience is flow.

Magic!

An example from my own life was not long ago I got an email that $500 had been deducted from my bank account through some online financial system.

I had no affiliation at all to where my money went. I tried to contact the only name in the email associated with the system and got no response. ZIP! $500 gone!

Did I get upset? No. I simply had a story. All I did was let go. That way I made sure I was not affected emotionally by it.

I emailed back to the name in the original email and let him know there had been a mistake. It took a couple of days for him to respond, and his response was to refund the money right back to my account.

This is just one simple example of hundreds. The bottom line here is, I had no problem because I had no emotion about it. I was in flow. This made the path to resolution clear and it resolved itself with ease.

Why?

Because life is all about "energy". The energy you feel is the energy you put out. It travels like waves from your "core" into your world. It sends signals and messages. And it organizes your life to match the signal or "who" you are being... your "identity".

Other people have the same kind of "core". They may or may not receive your signals depending on their "identity". But we all have the same thing working inside of us.

Your "core" or inner antenna is always communicating with your world. How to make that communication clear and effective is to make sure the "signal" is clear.

How to make the signal clear is to clear your spirit. Clear the baggage. Lighten your burdens. Release yourself from the pain and suffering. This is what allows the Magic to flow.

So let's go on and learn how to do The Core Method, clear the spirit and let the Magic flow!

Part Four

18

How to Do The Core Method

Now I'm going to take you through the steps of The Core Method. At first, it may seem a little complicated. Please be patient. Believe me when I say, once you understand it, you'll be able to do the method in seconds and experience real and powerful changes. First...

Identify the Story.
Think of something that bothers you. Whatever it is – it's a story in your life. An experience you've had or are having that you want to stop feeling bad about.

Something you want to be able to let go of. Once you have that story in mind...

Feel the Intensity Level.
Remember, you're only going to use this "zero" to "ten" scale as a beginner. Once you get used to the method, you won't need to use it anymore. It's just to make you more aware of the progress you achieve with the method in the beginning.

Notice how intense the emotion is that comes up. On the "zero" to "ten" scale, ten being the worst possible emotions about it, how high is that emotion on that scale? a five? a seven? a ten? This is your intensity number for that story.

Make a mental note of that intensity number and then set the story and number aside.

That story is now "intended".

Remember I said intention is "king"? This means your subconscious mind "knows" that's the story you are working on. It is assumed and understood. Just keep that intensity number in the back of your mind. Now, having set the story aside...

Focus on the Emotion.
What emotion do you feel in your body because of that story?

- Fear?
- Anger?
- Frustration?
- Guilt?
- Shame?
- Anxiety?
- Confusion?
- Something else?

Whatever the emotion is, that emotion is what's stuck in your body. That's what's causing you trouble. Not the story, but the emotion. Whatever the emotion is, it's pointing to what's missing for you about that story.

Define What's Missing.

No matter what the emotion is, it will always bring up one or more of three things. Wanting control, approval or safety. Not "having" them is that lack feeling. "Having" them is relief and freedom. Empowerment.

No matter what it's been in your life that you *wanted*:
- a new relationship
- to leave a bad relationship
- a car
- a home
- more money
- to not cry about that "thing" again
- to pay your bills

- to be healed
- to pass the test
- to get the job
- to win the game... whatever.

The feeling the emotion points to is "wanting" control, approval or safety. One or more of them is missing.

The Three Questions

How do you get to have what's missing?

Here's how...

Focus on the emotion that story causes you to feel and think about these three... "wanting control", "wanting approval" or "wanting safety or security".

As you do this, you'll get a "catch" or a "clutch" in your gut or somewhere in your body. A strong feeling about one of them. A "knowing" sense. A feeling in your body or gut that says... "That's the one! That's what's missing!"

When you feel the emotion and think of these three, you ask yourself the three questions...

"Does this *emotion* (name the emotion to yourself) bring up "Wanting control?"

You'll notice if that feels true.

If it doesn't, ask yourself...

"Does this *emotion* bring up "Wanting approval?"

If that doesn't feel true, then ask...

"Does this *emotion* bring up "Wanting safety or security?"

You'll "know"when you focus on the right one.

You'll get a sense of a "YES!" feeling that says, "That's the one"!

It's the same feeling you get when you absolutely know you are right about something or when you speak a powerful truth.

This is your body's natural strong/weak response. Your subconscious mind holds your truth, whatever that may be. When you speak or think something your subconscious knows is true for you, it responds in your body with a strong feeling.

Like when you say, "My name is..." and then say your real name. You've spoken a truth that your subconscious recognizes and in response, gives your body a charge of strength.

Like when your team scores a touchdown or you get the big promotion or you finally pay off your house or car. It's like that feeling.

As a test for yourself, say, "My name is..." and say your real name. Notice how you feel in your body. To compare, now say, "My name is..." and say a name that is not yours and notice the difference in how you feel in your body. There will be a felt sense of a change in your overall state of being. You'll go from a feeling of winning the game to that feeling of losing the game.

We all know the difference in how this feels. This is your body responding to a positive and a negative. It does the same with a truth and something that is not true. This is why muscle testing works.

Truth is a strong feeling. Untruth is a weak feeling.

When you think of a truth, something inside your body just feels congruent and strong. One or more of the three, "wanting control", "wanting approval" or "wanting safety", will give you this strong feeling. You may even feel all of them do this.

In this case, just pick one and do the method to release "wanting" that thing... control, approval or safety so you can default into "having" it. At that point, it won't matter which one you release first because in a few seconds, you can use the method on the others if you need to.

Also, you'll quickly become so used to the three questions that you won't have to go through this formal questioning process. You'll simply think of each one, "control, approval or safety", and in that moment, you'll "know". You'll feel it.

Now, I prefer to use muscle testing to get my answers. It's more clear, and direct. Especially when you start looking for answers about your life, what happened, how you felt about all that and the decisions that resulted.

If you haven't quite got it yet, pay close attention to your *feelings*. That will work for this simple process of determining what you want...

Control – Approval – Safety

Experience Your Core

Most of the time we are awake, our awareness is directed out into the world. Rarely do we actually direct our awareness into our own body to get a sense of what it feels like in there. We are aware of our physical sensations, emotions and feelings which are in our bodies, but we generally do this and then make some kind of assessment or judgment about it which puts us back in our heads.

It's a very different experience when you get the feeling someone is watching you. You become aware of a sensation you're not familiar with because someone else's awareness is on you. It's weird, but it happens. The thing is, most people do not know they can do the same thing to themselves.

The difference is, when someone is watching you, there is simply an awareness that this is happening. When *you watch you*, this becomes a connection between your own mind and the core of your body. When done with specific intention, you can accomplish life changing things.

I am now going to direct you to have an experience of your core. I suggest you read this part a bit slower and actually do as instructed so you can experience your core. You just might feel something you've never felt before.

The core of your body is a line dividing your body vertically into two halves, left from right, from your tailbone up your spine and your neck to the top of your head. Now let's go deep...

Being quiet and focusing...

Take a moment - be aware of your awareness.

You can direct your awareness as you read.

Put your awareness at your navel.

Move your awareness inside your body, back to your spine.

Move your awareness up your spine to the center of your body.

Your awareness is in your core at the level of your solar plexus.

Let your awareness be there for a moment or two.

Notice how it feels to be in your core.

Your awareness is how you experience your entire world.

Now you are experiencing you.

Like when you get the feeling someone is watching you.

YOU... are watching you.

Now come back to normal awareness.

As you did this, your awareness established a special connection with your core. A communication with your inner self. And the intention will always be - Peace. Healing. Release. Freedom. Having.

If you have followed my instructions, you are now aware of this connection. Much is said about head and heart communication. You have just established this communication. It will serve you well in The Core Method. Read on.

Doing The Core Method

Let's say for example, the story you're working on makes you feel angry. As a result, you get a feeling in your body that this anger you are experiencing causes you to feel like you want "control".

You're angry about something that happened...
- This generally means you *want* control.
- You feel you lost control when it happened.
- It took control from you and now you *want* it back.
- You feel "wanting".

Hold that thought in your mind... "Wanting control".

As you hold that thought, direct your awareness into the center of your body down low, back at your spine, down close to your tailbone.

While thinking, "Wanting control", scan your awareness up your spine, up your neck and out the top of your head all in about two or three seconds. That's all it takes. Take a breath, let it out and relax.

Your spine is the "core" of your body with its four highly sensitive systems. Your awareness is the powerful element you can place in or on things and affect them.

You've established a connection between your awareness and your "core" or your mind and heart. They know what to do. They are aware as you read. The "core" of your body is the "center" of your feeling experience of your life. Your point of access to release all negative emotions by releasing "wanting" so you feel "having".

Like I've been saying, the story is not the problem.

"Wanting" is the problem. "Having" is the solution.

"Having" is always better than "wanting" because "having" is the "emotional" experience of completion, fulfillment, wholeness, ownership, success. It's OK to "have" in life. And if you ever feel like it's not... do the method.

You must understand that like all of your emotional states, both of these, "wanting" and "having", are simply psycho-emotional or energetic-psychological states.

They are both "energy".
Like even though you may own a car and can go out and drive it around, you still have the energetic "feeling" experience of ownership of the car in your body as an emotion.

There's a strong sense of rightness to owning that car. But it's a feeling. An emotional state. You experience both of these, "wanting" and "having", as feelings or emotional states.

What's more, your experience of "wanting" can easily be changed to "having" by directing your awareness (which is energy) into your core, which is extremely sensitive to energy, with the specific intention (which is energy) of letting go of the "wanting" state (which is energy) so you can automatically default into the "having" state. (which is energy) Get it?

When you do The Core Method as described here, something unexplainable (magical?) happens that causes you to release the "wanting" state, and automatically default into the "having" state.

This means in that moment, you will generally feel a shift in your body. Something in your "feeling" sense will change for you about that emotion and story and you'll recognize it. You'll have a felt sense of change.

I have no explanation for why this change occurs, but it does. Even I am quite amazed that our bodies and minds are designed and can work this way. All this time we have been carrying around the answer to all the problems of our lives and we didn't know it!

What's more, because you can only exist in one or the other of these two states, "wanting" or "having", the default change will always put you into the positive state because it simply does not work in reverse.

In other words, you can't hurt yourself or make yourself feel bad with The Core Method. It's just not possible.

So when you release the emptiness of "wanting" control, approval or safety, the only other state left that you could possibly experience is the default state of "having" them.

The core of your body feels the "wanting" feeling. Your intention is to release "wanting". Your awareness is the tool you use to deliver the instruction, (intention) or the "OK" to your core to make the emotional change in your body.

You put your awareness into your core, back at your spine, down at your tailbone and as you do this, think the thought... "Wanting control" or whichever you feel is the one. This is your intention.

Then scan your awareness up your spine, up your neck and out the top of your head all in three or four seconds. This is the action that makes the change. This is the center of The Core Method. I can't explain why it works, but it does! This is the essence of and doorway to your own Authentic Magic!

The Core Method Review

Now that you've done the method, go back to the story you were working on and review it.

Notice how you feel when you think about it. Does it still feel the same, or did the intensity of the emotion about that story drop down?

If it was a seven on the scale before, is it now a five? A four? A two? Or is it completely gone?

If there's any of the feeling or emotion left, focus into the rest of it and feel it. Do the method on the rest of it until it's gone. Also, if there is any of it left, notice if the "want" is still the same. Or did it change?

Notice if it changed and if needed, redo the method with the new "want". If it was "wanting control" but now feels more like "wanting approval", do the method on that. If it's "wanting safety", then do that.

Do the method by focusing on the "wanting" and clear the rest of this emotion. Since it only takes a few seconds to do the method, it's easy to go through it two or three times in a minute to clear an emotion.

Again I'll remind you, the more you use The Core Method, the better it works. Continued use means you'll soon be able to eliminate just about any negative emotion in one application of the method.

Along with this thought may come the realization that there isn't a single negative emotion you have to put up with if you don't want to because you now know how to eliminate any one of them in seconds.

Period.

Bad Habits

The more you use the method, the better it works. Yes, I know, I keep pointing this out. It's because I'm trying to plant the idea in your mind to develop the habit of turning to The Core Method to deal with your life instead of coping with it using any old bad habits.

I also point this out because not everyone is built psychologically or programmed the same way inside. Not everyone comes from the same experiences of life or has the same temperament or beliefs about how things work in their world.

What you are doing by using this method is establishing a new way to communicate with your subconscious mind. You are directly addressing the very structure of your values, beliefs, attitudes, opinions and judgments. Your very "identity"!

What is that structure? It's "energy".

You are addressing these structures with more "energy"... your *awareness and intention*. Be patient. Your subconscious mind learns quickly. It's your conscious mind I'm talking to right now. This can be a new thing for your conscious mind if you are unfamiliar with energetic processes.

Turn to The Core Method to improve your life by using it as often as possible on everything that makes you feel less than good.

The thing is, most people never do this. They generally tend to "cope" with their problems with their favorite bad habit. I call any coping mechanism a bad habit because if you do it to keep from feeling, it's not helping you. It's hurting you. Whatever one uses to try to push their emotions back down inside so they can try to ignore them is a bad habit.

Coping of any kind ends up being a bad habit. The big problem with this is the subconscious mind loves habits. Why? Because they are comfortable. Why are they comfortable? Because they are "familiar". And the familiar is comfortable... even if it's bad for you!

Again, the subconscious mind does not decide this. You have to make the conscious decision to eliminate the bad stuff from your life.

Doing them over and over is how they become habits. And it's so easy to fall back into old habits when you're trying to make changes in your life. In fact, you may "know" about this. Just know that you can also create a good habit too.

Remember, your subconscious mind runs about 90% of your life.

What's comfortable may not be good for you. I'm just making you aware and giving you the tools to make change more easily and encouraging you to make a habit of it.

While your subconscious mind holds your survival instincts, when it comes to bad habits, it's like the frog in the pot analogy. The frog in the pot sitting on the stove is in cool water at first. But turn the fire on and the water gradually heats up. However, the frog is too comfortable in the water.

A little warmth is ok. But eventually, the frog will boil to death because the change is slow and gradual. It's not uncomfortable enough to jump out. It's easier to stay in the familiar pot than make a change. People with their habits can be a lot like that frog. Don't be a frog!

Remember, you've established a connection between your awareness and your core. This is experienced as a comforting thing to your subconscious mind. Releasing will be easy because of this connection. The subconscious mind is a quick study.

Keep using the method until you can think of "that story" and feel nothing for it. This is the goal of The Core Method.

When that happens, you are becoming what's called, "imperturbable". This is where nothing and no one bothers you. Does this mean you become numb to life? Not at all! You just have a choice now whether you want to go on suffering or be free.

As you do the method on more and more of the stories in your life, you are becoming more imperturbable. You are clearing your energy blocks and becoming more emotionally, psychologically and energetically free with every application of the method.

You are empowering yourself to create your life the way you would "have" it be, not how you "want" it to be. In other words, you are allowing the Authentic Magic of your spirit to flow in your life.

19

Techniques to Empower The Core Method

Technique #1

Here's a technique I use that will help you focus your awareness even more powerfully into your core as you do the method.

Have you ever noticed how you feel when someone points a finger at you? Really gets your attention, right? Pointing is a powerful technique. One you can use to make The Core Method work even better.

When you close the fingers of either hand against your palm, your fingers are pointing back at you. Bend your wrist a little and point your fingers right at your core where your awareness is.

The moment you begin the scan up your spine or core, point the fingers of either hand at your tailbone and then move your hand, with fingers pointing at your core, up your spine as your awareness tracks along. Move them up your spine together.

Sometimes as you scan up the spine, you may feel like moving a bit more slowly in certain places. There may be times when you notice you feel the intensity of the release more in one location along the spine than in others.

This is because you are also tracking along the chakra points which connect to the spine on one end and energetically to the different organs of the body on the other end through the energy meridians.

According to Chinese acupuncture, each organ of the body has its own emotional tendencies. This means each organ tends to hold onto specific emotions we may have experienced in life that we didn't process effectively.

When you direct your awareness into these locations along your spine where the chakras connect, the emotions may intensify in certain places. Pointing at that location with your fingers intensifies the release of that emotion from that chakra and organ.

Your awareness is a powerful energy. When directed inside with intention, it stimulates the release of the emotions connected to the chakras and organs you're directing your awareness to.

This pointing technique is very powerful and can add measurable effectiveness or a "felt sense" of change to your experience of the method.

Doing the method can also improve the health of the organs you release old emotions from. Releasing energy blocks allows your body's energy system to flow more smoothly which brings life force and healing to your internal organs and entire body.

Technique #2

I've worked with a few people who had trouble seeing or visualizing mental pictures. This makes it hard to see their spine in their mind's eye. But even though some people do not see images in their imaginations, they can sense a scene and describe it.

This is why if you ask a person who does not see mental images to describe their living room, they can do it. And this is why not being able to see mental images is not a problem.

When this is the case, they can generally still do the method as described. If not, I may direct them to focus inside of their body and imagine a fluorescent light tube running up their spine.

Everyone knows what a fluorescent light looks like. The moment they direct their awareness inside their body, they can simply sense that fluorescent tube flashing on brightly and lighting up their spine from the bottom of their tailbone to top of their head for just a few seconds.

This does the same thing as scanning up their spine because your awareness is on your entire lighted spine at the same time.

Your "awareness" of this flash of "light" in your spine causes the release in that moment because your awareness is in your spine or "core" at the same time. This works amazingly well if you don't see images in your imagination.

Once you've done this, stop, take a breath, let it out and get quiet. Go back to the story and play it. See if you can bring up any emotion. If you get any little bit of it to come up, just do the light tube again.

And the same goes for this technique... the more you use it, the better it works. If you will do this, pretty soon using the method becomes second nature or a useful "habit" and you'll find yourself applying it on almost everything.

As a result, your life will begin flowing more smoothly every day. This is when the Authentic Magic begins to show up in your life.

The Magical State

Some things to understand about yourself...
1. Energy flows where awareness goes.
2. Your "core" lights up when awareness is on it.
3. The "essential you" is awareness which is energy.
4. Energy, which is you, attracts 24 hours a day.
5. You are a COE or the "Center Of Energy" in your world.
6. Your thoughts, pictures and emotions are your "energy".
7. You are in control of the quality of your "energy".
8. The quality of your energy determines your "state of being".
9. Your "state of being" determines your power to manifest.
10. Your "highest power" is the "Magical State of Being".
11. The "Magical State" is the state of "having".
12. You automatically default into the state of "having" when you do the method.

The "having" state sets your emotional state and the overall tone of your life to a felt sense of ownership and success, which is the energy or feeling of confidence, of knowing, of completion and peace.

The confident energy you put out travels like waves and will affect your world energetically and return that energy multiplied which makes your path to success much easier. In fact, your plan or goal may manifest in an even better way than you imagined.

Think about it... say you're worried about passing an important exam at school or doing well at an interview for a great job or impressing that special someone. What's the most common state you might be in before the exam or interview? A little anxious? Nervous? Worried you won't pass? Hoping you will pass? Afraid the boss won't like you? Hoping that special someone likes you?

These kinds of thoughts are very common in scenarios like these. And what is this? It's focusing on what you don't want. It's not "having"! It's saying, "No". It's "wanting"!

Do you remember what the subconscious mind does with this? It magnifies and multiplies your state and gives you more of what you're focused on.

Like that famous bible quote says, "My greatest fear hath befallen me!" Fear is simply a lot of intense focus on something you don't want. Something you are resisting... failure.

"Like attracts like."
This is the law. You don't get what you want.
You get who you are.

If you're scared you'll fail, that's who you're *being*. As a result, chances are good you will fail. And then you do. And you think it's fate.

No! It's not! You are powerful and can create the good... AND the bad! Most people just hate taking responsibility for this fact.

Now, try again. Only this time, do The Core Method on your emotions about the test or interview or that big date or performance or whatever. If you got the job or passed the interview, if you were successful, how would you feel?

Complete! Whole! Confident! Like a winner! Or, in other words... you'd *have* what you set your mind to, right?

Why not just go right straight to that state and bring it with you? "Be" the one who passed the test or got the job before you even go there.

The Magical State is where you've already won! You are already in the completed frame of mind and emotion. This way, you go in with confidence. You already "own" this test or interview or whatever you've chosen to have. And that energy goes before you and affects your world and experience.

- Do you feel doubt? That's "wanting". Do the method.
- Do you hope? That's "wanting". Do the method.
- Are you nervous? That's "wanting". Do the method.

Do it on every little aspect of your intention and assume the Magical State of "ownership"... "having"! Because when you own something, game over! You've won!

By the way... If it doesn't turn out how you planned, do the method. This will clear your path to something even better than you planned. Trust me when I say... it's out there. Doing the method is how you remain clear so what you've chosen can come in through an even better path.

This has happened to me many times. Jobs came easily, after a car accident, the new car that came in, after money disappeared from my bank account, it came back, random money showing up, moving to a new state and finding a place to live quickly, even easily resolved health issues. Lots of examples of things Magically working themselves out. And without stress, or as I like to say... "with ease".

You have this ability now. You have The Core Method.

Part Five

20

Other Important Concepts

This book is teaching you how to do The Core Method. Although there seems to be a lot to all this, it's really a very simple method once you get the basics.

The simple steps are:
- Think of the story.
- Feel the emotion.
- Ask yourself which "wanting" the emotion brings up – "wanting" control, approval or safety.
- Put your awareness into your center or core.
- Say "Wanting control" (or whichever applies)
- Scan your awareness up your spine holding that thought in mind.
- Stop and take a breath.
- Now check back with the story and see if it still has the same intensity, or has it come down... or dissolved completely?

There it is in a nutshell. Eight little steps you can do all in about ten or fifteen seconds. The actual scan up the spine only takes a few seconds. That's it. But like chess, getting good at the method will take time and experience.

I say this because the number of ways you can apply the method to yourself and your life is limitless. So be patient. We human beings are very complex creatures. The subconscious mind makes all kinds of connections you aren't even aware of. Lots of little things come up daily that you can use the method on. Some of it may take longer to show up. But things will come up as you're ready to release them.

A lot of your emotional reactions to the stories of your life will come up whether you like it or not. That's just life. These emotions are making it easy for you to find them. They volunteer themselves when something happens that connects to an old memory.

But we all have a lot of "stuff" we deal with that may not be so apparent. We even have "stuff" we don't want to admit to. This means looking within and searching out the problems that trouble you. Most people don't want to go looking for trouble. This is why I say...

"Every emotion that comes up is basically asking your permission to leave."

True story! Most people do not have a method like is taught here, so they end up coping with their emotions in the hope that those emotions will somehow leave them alone if they push them back down inside far enough.

Of course that's never the case. Emotions shoved back down inside are still very much alive and will eventually force you to pay attention to them. Either in bad behavior, pain and loss or disease... or... all the above.

Just know that the possibilities available to you now are beyond your comprehension at this moment. I made a collection of things one can work on. It's a list of many hundreds of possibilities. I call it "The Issues List". I finally quit adding to it when I realized there is no end to what can be worked on, but I wanted to share some of it, so here is...

A Short List of Things You Might Let Go of...

I've pointed out that learning The Core Method is like learning to play chess. It's easy enough to learn how to play, but getting good at the game takes time and experience. Knowing what you can apply the method to is like that.

This is why I want to give you some ideas or thoughts that you might consider looking into concerning your life. I have no idea what your life has been like. But if you are a normal human being, there's a chance you've dealt with one or more issues related to something on this list.

This list is a tiny fraction of my original "Issues List". Going through it might help you to remember what stories you have hidden, or maybe not so hidden, in your mind and deeper self.

As you scan down the list, notice if you have any reaction whatsoever to any item on it. That will be an obvious indication that there is something going on for you in that area. Explore it and do the method on all that comes up... "wanting" control, approval, safety. They are in no particular order.

P.S. I realize this list may be pretty blunt for some people. My apologies. But sometimes blunt honesty is needed in order to confront the truth buried deep inside before it can be released.

P.S.S. No one is watching. It's OK. K? ♥

Ready? Go...

Hate - Anger - Betrayed - Abandoned - Love - Fear - Abused - Stupid - Unloved - Brother - Terror - Used - Uncle - Shame - Guilt - Cousin - Rape - Big Trouble - Boyfriend - Inlaws - Despair - Worry - Fretting - I can't - I won't - Father - I'll never - Worthless - Powerless - Foreboding - Mother - Insincere - Dishonest - Perfectionist - Stepfather - Neighbor - Shunned - Inferior - Work - Insanity - Relationships - Women - Embarrassed - Quitter - Stuck - Unwanted - Confused - Rejected - Depression - Men - Sadness - Aunt - Lonely - Incapable - Unlovable - Ignored - Grief - Anxiety - Hopless - Sister - Hurt - Dispair - Rejection - Lieing - Judgment - Dependency - Girlfriend - Inferior - Incest - Stepmother - Parents - Crash - Divorce - Death - Resentment - Bitterness - Molested - Wrecked - Controlled - Incompetent - Incapable - Judged - Unforgiveness - Cast out - Disowned

This is what I mean about getting good at the game. For a lot of people, this list will give them something to remember and use the method on. Or it will remind them of things not on this list that maybe they had forgotten. Something buried deep in their psyche that's still affecting them and they don't realize it.

Yeah, that happens a lot. Do the method.

The flow of your Magic depends on letting go of as much of this kind of stuff as you can. The Core Method will make this possible. Just be willing to go for it. And if you feel any hesitancy, do the method on that first. It will work.

Blessings to you and those you love. They will benefit from your willingness and growth.

21

Secondary Gain

After working with many people to help them overcome their own difficulties in life, I realized that my favorite personal approach was to teach others the method I used, take them through a few experiences of using it and then encourage them to continue to do their own work.

This is because I feel it empowers them to take control of their own lives. I also work this way because I don't want to be the "deal" in people's lives. In other words, I don't want to be your "guru" or perceived as your "healer" who has you coming back again and again.

> **"I want you to be able to do your own work even when I'm not there."**

This just makes sense to me.

But as I did the work with others and taught classes, I realized that there are those who care enough to do the work for themselves, and there are those who seem to get caught up in their lives and fall back into their old habits of forgetting and coping.

I will always remember the experience I had with one lady long ago who was on Facebook complaining about her life. I offered to teach her how to do the method. She was interested in the help, so I taught her.

A few weeks later I saw her back on Facebook complaining about something else in her life. I messaged her and asked her if she tried to use the method I taught her. Her reply was, "Oh, I forgot". I took that to mean she didn't really want to be healed. She preferred to complain.

The preference to complain generally means there is some kind of benefit or as psychologists call it, "secondary gain", from complaining. Often people prefer to tell their stories over and over to themselves and anyone who will listen. Misery loves company?

The payoff may be the attention, empathy, sympathy or maybe a sense of importance or whatever. Just know that the ego loves to be stroked and if you get sympathy or any of that by telling your stories, that's what's happening.

It's my hallucination that people are actually trying to get "approval" or love this way because that's the "wanting" they are experiencing. But this is not healthy and indicates one needs to go inside and look for "what's missing".

> *"All of our painful stories, no matter how deeply they are buried or how much we talk about them, will bring up "wanting" either control, approval or safety. "*

When you figure it out, do the method.

Skeptical The Method Will Work For You?

At this point, I'll add a little trick I use with some people. It's somewhat common for people who are unfamiliar with energy psychology modalities to be skeptical of their efficacy.

In other words, it might be hard for some people to believe this simple little trick of the mind can make their very real negative emotions disappear so easily. I mean, they've likely cultivated them for a long time and are quite invested.

Know what I mean? Yeah.

And I understand. This is why sometimes, when needed, one of the first issues I work on with these people is their "skepticism" or feelings of doubt about the method.

For example, I have experienced this when I'm invited to go to a person's house to work with the lady of the house and her husband is there to observe.

As I'm working with her and he is watching, I can tell he thinks it's all a bunch of bull. I mean, there is some serious eyebrow raising going on over there. Meanwhile, his wife is getting great results and he can see how impressed she is. This creates a bit of cognitive dissonance for him.

This one time, after she had gotten emotional relief, she said to her husband, "Honey, why don't you let him try this on that thing? You know... that thing you deal with".

He's like, "I don't know."

So I said, "You're skeptical this works, right?"

And of course the answer is yes. So I tell him to notice his skeptical feelings. "Skepticism has a feeling to it. Can you feel it?" He answers, "Yes".

So I encourage him to just try it on that feeling. He has no ego about his skepticism. But he does about this silly Jedi mind trick. Within minutes, his skepticism is gone and I'm working on "that thing" with him. And it works!

Every thought has an associated "feeling" to it. This includes doubt. You know it when you feel it. This is because in between your conscious and subconscious minds is what's called the "critical factor". The guard at the gate of your mind that doesn't let you fall for just any 'ol thing.

If you doubt that this Core Method is "all that", your critical factor has kicked in. What you're seeing does not match your model of the world. It's just a case of cognitive dissonance. If this is the case, the first thing to eliminate is your skepticism or doubt.

Experience has taught me over and over that when you sincerely apply the method to your doubt, it will reduce or eliminate it. Then you can go on and eliminate the more important and troubling issues in your life. Just follow the same instructions for doubt as for any emotion. It will work.

22

An Interesting Secret About Your Emotions

"Every negative emotion wants out."

Meaning, every troubling emotion wants out of your body and experience. In fact, when negative emotions come up and you feel them, they are essentially asking your permission to leave. They do not come up just to give you a bad time.

Your subconscious mind is very aware of your negative emotions and is also aware of how much better off you'd be if they were released and gone. Your stories bring up your emotions so you can process them.

And you must give them your permission. Weird, huh?

Your emotions cannot randomly leave your experience unless you specifically do something to allow this to happen. It's a control element the subconscious mind uses to prevent emotional chaos.

Most of the time we do not give our emotions permission to leave because we have no idea we can do this. We just feel bad and curse our problem so it tends to stick with us until we do something that we hope will change our experience.

You know, therapy, drugs, burning bowl ceremony, some kind of ritual, screaming into a pillow, etc. In my experience with people, these methods rarely work long term. In a day or three, they'll be right back where they were before... cursing their problem and going back to their therapist again. And again. And again. Ugh!

The truth is, when we feel an emotion about a problem of any kind, physical or emotional, it simply wants to exit the premises. Leave. Evaporate.

True story.

Doing the method is the perfect way to give your negative emotions your permission. The bad habit of coping is like saying, "No" which keeps you stuck. Doing the method is saying, "Yes" which is freedom.

It not only works, the changes you will make will be about 95% permanent. The other 5% quite often comes from not addressing the problem in a way that the subconscious mind recognizes as valid.

Check again and apply The Core Method in a slightly different way. You'll likely get it.

23

Metaphors for The Core Method

The Emotional Computing Metaphor

Think of a negative emotion as a virus, document or file in your computer. When you want to delete any of these from your computer, you click "delete".

What pops up?

A box that says, "Are you sure you want to delete this?" At this point, you have a choice to make... "Yes" or "No". You must click "Yes" for it to leave your computer, right?

You must give it your "permission" to leave your computer or you might inadvertently cause damage you don't want to have to deal with. Your emotional self works basically the same way.

Saying or clicking "No" is how to keep a problem in your computer. When you have an emotional or financial or whatever problem and disapprove of it, complain about it or cope with it, you are basically saying "No" to it. Meaning, "No, you can't leave."

Same goes for ignoring it, medicating it, eating to make it go away, shopping, sex, drugs and any other means one might employ to shove the bad feelings back down.

This is just like clicking "No" in your computer when you are given the choice to delete something. This means it stays in your computer to cause further trouble. Emotions do the same thing.

When you click "Yes", it leaves your computer and is no longer a problem. When you use The Core Method to release the emotions around a physical or emotional problem, you are essentially saying "Yes" and giving your emotions your permission to leave and they do so quite happily and instantly.

The Giant Amazon in the Sky Metaphor

The Universe will deliver whatever you own. But you must come into the state of ownership for this to happen. Amazon is a perfect example of this.

Here's how it works... You know what you want. That's called desire. You're in a state of "wanting" that thing. Remember, "wanting" is not "having"? So you go to Amazon and find it.

Once you've clicked all the right buttons and submitted your order, your state changes. Now you're in the "Magical State". You're in the state of "ownership". You now have the right to fully expect delivery of your chosen item, right?

You may not have it in your hands yet, but now you have a sense of confidence you didn't have before your order was placed. Now you "own" it.

Now think about this...

Do you try to control "how" it gets to you? No! That's not your job! You confidently allow Amazon to handle that.

Do you try to make the delivery happen faster than is possible? No! That's not your job either! You sit back and relax knowing Amazon will deliver your item in a timely manner.

Your Job?

"Decide what you want and place your order."

That's it! That's how you become the owner of what you choose for yourself on Amazon. Choose it and order it. Once you place your order, it belongs to you and now your state has changed to "ownership".

When it comes to attracting into your life the things, people and experiences you choose, how do you order it? You release "wanting" it so you naturally default into a state of "having" it. That's how you order anything from the Universe!

Think about it... that whole "wanting" and "having" thing even works with Amazon! You either *want* that item... or you *have* it! Placing your order is establishing ownership which is "having"!

This works with everything in your life because all "wanting" calls for control, approval and safety. When you do the method, you go from "wanting" something to the energetic state of "having" it. Your subconscious mind takes over from there and the Universe delivers it. Doubts are gone. Confidence is at its peak. The state of "having" is The Magic!

Amazon's job?

Take responsibility for how it will get to you and make this happen in a timely manner. Cut and dried. Same goes for the Universe and the creative process! Place your order with the Universe by changing your state and the Universe will deliver!

Manifesting only calls for you to do two things... choose what you will have – and order it... or in other words... release "wanting" it and assume the Magical State of "having" it. The rest is not your job! Let the professionals do their job and you do yours. The Universe is a professional! It knows what to do when your order is placed correctly. Now you know what to do too!

24

Disapproval? Beat Yourself Up!
This Equals Self Destruction!

This is one of the biggest and MOST damaging things we all do! For example, when you can't get what you want, you disapprove of yourself and what happened and then you beat yourself up.

When you do something stupid, (by your judgment) you disapprove of yourself and then beat yourself up, or put yourself down.

Even more, whenever you don't like what someone else has said or done or you don't like some situation or group, you may very well disapprove of them or it and then mentally and emotionally beat them up.

All feelings of disapproval end up with you beating yourself or someone else up because disapproving of anything is a negative thought. And here is the kicker… our own conscience will hold that thought against us.

Did you get that?

Disapproving of yourself or anyone or anything and beating yourself or them up is a negative thought and your conscience or subconscious mind will tend to hold that thought in a light that somehow, you were bad for thinking that way. Then it tends to become a karma thing that must be settled or balanced. (Stay tuned. I will be covering karma soon.)

For the most part, the ego will try to justify this thinking so you can feel OK about beating yourself or someone else up, which pretty much never works at your deeper levels of being. This is because your spirit or deeper self knows better. It holds your sense of morality and you may not consciously know how deep that goes.

Here's a hint... you get a little kick in the guts when you do something that goes against your deeper morality. The problem is, if you persist in this thinking or activity, the kick will eventually stop. But your deeper self will still keep score on all of it.

Since the ego loves conflict, even with yourself, it will tell you to beat yourself up, which is something the ego loves but yet, is a very unloving thing to do. Remember, the Magic of life is all about love. Especially self love. This is how you get the Magic flowing in your life.

The idea of The Core Method is to eliminate all unloving thoughts, emotions and feelings because they are all blocks to your Magic. Whenever you catch yourself being unforgiving or disapproving or beating yourself up, that's a call for you to change that part of you.

Let it all go by doing the method.

Pay attention to your thoughts and feelings. They will tell you when you feel bad about a thought. When you feel that way, do the method. Hold the thought in mind. What does it bring up? Wanting control, approval or safety? Carry that thought into your center and scan up. Take a breath. Check again.

See how easy that is?

It's Not OK!

Sometimes letting go of an emotion is hard to do because there are hidden reasons to hang onto it. A simple example would be the difficulty one has in letting go of the feelings of animosity toward an ex-relationship with a person, group or organization.

Even a rude driver on the road!

You are done with the relationship or encounter and have tried to let go and move on but something is making it hard to let go of the anger or grudge and it keeps popping up and you don't know why.

I have worked with women who can't forgive their ex because of the pain the ex caused her. She can't let go because she doesn't realize she has a hidden rule about fairness. It's simply "not OK" with her to let him off so easy. She wants her "pound of flesh" so to speak, but she doesn't recognize this about herself. She's just stuck in her anger and can't seem to let go.

In this case, always look for a preliminary or hidden step or rule or "hidden qualifier" you have unconsciously set up for this person or this kind of situation. This makes it necessary to back up a step before you can move forward with successful releasing.

I call it, "It's Not OK..."

If you feel stuck and can't let go, hold the person or situation in mind and allow the emotions to come up and address it by saying or think something like this...

"It's not OK with me to let this person off so easily because they don't deserve forgiveness".

"It's not OK with me that he/she/they cheated me out of "X" and there's nothing I can do about it".

"It's not OK with me to let this go because it's like letting them win and I get nothing".

"It's not OK with me to let this go because they haven't suffered enough for the pain they caused me".

"It's not OK with me that the kids, husband, boss, company, kids at school, teacher, etc. disrespects me".

"It's not OK to forgive when I feel so disrespected."

"It's not OK that he/she cheated on me."

"It's not OK with me to let go of this frustration/anger because they haven't changed and they probably never will".

One of these or something similar may very well be what's got you stuck. There are any number of qualifiers one might create for a situation or relationship. If you get a strong feeling on something like this about a story, you have a hidden rule about letting go of it or that person. This "Not Ok-ness" will keep you stuck. Get the idea?

Some part of you has set some kind of qualification the other must fulfill before you can allow them to just walk away scot-free... or in other words, before you can fully let go and be done with the situation. Some part of you just can't let go until this qualification has been met or fulfilled.

Releasing these qualifiers and needing anything else from them before you can let go is often all you have to do. Addressing the qualifiers can lead to other realizations. Let go of these and the rest of your work will go more easily.

Just do the method on the qualifiers the same way as for any emotion. When you do this, letting go of the rest of the story will come much easier.

This also works with many other things.
A few examples might be:
"It's not OK with me to not have enough money."
"It's not OK with me that my car is broken down."
"It's not OK with me to fail this exam/interview."
"It's not OK with me that I'm sick right now."
"It's not OK with me that he/she hasn't called."
"It's not OK with me that I don't have a relationship like I thought I would by now."
"It's not OK with me that I can't afford to _____."
"It's not OK with me that I'm overweight."
"It's not OK with me that I'm losing my hair."
"It's not OK with me that my eyesight/hearing is going bad."
"It's not OK with me that I embarrassed myself in front of my friends."
"It's not OK with me to speak in front of a crowd of people."
"It's not OK with me that I get confused and don't know what to do."
"It's not OK with me when my plans fell apart."

Etc... By the way, this also works on your karma. That section comes later and if it's a problem, come back and read this section again. Whenever you have difficulty letting go of something, look for the qualifiers. Look for what's Not OK with you about it. Let that go first and the rest should go easier.

Other Reasons You Might Not Be Able to Let Go

Sometimes the very act of letting go of a problem has its own issues. This list gives you more resources to delve into your own mind and heart and discover the blocks to your Magic. If any of these below hold a charge of any kind for you, simply do the method on it just the same as anything else. They are all stories.

- I'll feel deprived if I get over this problem.
- It isn't right for me to just let this go.
- I want justice and if I just let this go, I won't get justice!
- I'll feel cheated if I just let this go.
- I want them to suffer the way I have suffered before I let this go.
- It's not fair for them to go off and live happily while I still hurt.
- What if I just let this go and then it happens again?
- I don't trust that letting this problem go will change anything.
- I don't trust myself to get over this problem.
- I don't trust others to help me get over this problem.
- I'm too embarrassed to get over this problem.
- God will not forgive me if I just let go of this problem.
- I can't let go of this problem because if I do, "X" will happen.
- I don't have the right to get over this problem.
- I'm not worthy enough to just let this problem go.
- I don't deserve to get over this problem.
- I deserve to suffer because of this problem.
- I'm afraid to get over this problem.
- I'll lose control of the problem if I just let it go.
- Getting over this problem will cause more problems.
- Others won't let me get over this problem.
- I don't believe in this method of getting over this problem.
- I don't want this method to work.

- I don't have any intention of getting over this problem.
- I need this problem because it justifies my anger. (Or other emotion.)
- This problem is too severe/too big to get over.
- I'm not capable of getting over this problem.
- I'm too angry (or other emotion) to get over this problem.
- They will take advantage of me if I get over this problem.
- Having this problem helps me stay angry at those responsible.
- I need my anger about this problem to be strong.
- I'm too intolerant to get over this problem.
- I'm too guilty to get over this problem.
- I don't love and accept myself enough to get over this problem.
- I have too many problems and limitations to get over this problem.
- I want or even need to keep all these problems.
- I will never get over this problem.
- It isn't safe for me to get over this problem.
- It isn't possible for me to get over this problem.
- I won't allow myself to get over this problem.
- Getting over this problem won't be good for me.
- Getting over this problem won't be good for others.
- I have a unique block to getting over this problem.

Did I mention what complex creatures we human beings are? Yeah. People can have the most amazing reasons for holding onto problems. I wonder if any of these in the list above gave you a little kick in the gut. If they did, just do the method on them. Then do it on the other real problems you deal with. The method will work on all of it.

25

The Three Hidden Qualifiers

This is probably one of the most important concepts you can get from this book.

If you can grasp these three things, look at your life and see where they affect you, and then use the method to eliminate them, you will be light years ahead in the emotional clearing and Authentic Magic game.

We have many conscious, personal and even hidden reasons why we do things, why we don't do things, and why we fail at doing things. But there are three major "hidden" qualifiers that are pretty common to all of us.

When we consider all that we choose to be, do and have in life, we may not realize we have put conditions on our ability to make these things happen for us. This is because as we live our lives, we develop beliefs that may be working against us and we don't know it.

Three of these beliefs are what I call, "qualifiers" because if you have these beliefs set in your deeper self and you don't measure up, you will fail. And the problem is, they are generally hidden from our conscious awareness.

The first of these three qualifiers is...

"Do I Deserve It?"

Deserving is a Fairness issue.

This basically means, "Have I paid the price for it?" "Have I suffered enough for it?" "Have I given up enough for it?" "Have I sacrificed enough for it?" "Have I educated myself properly for it?" "Do others agree I deserve it?". "Will others be angry if I achieve it?" Etc.

The second one is...

"Am I Worthy Of It?"

Being Worthy is a Morals issue.
It can mean things like, "Am I of the right character?" "Am I clean or pure enough?" "Do I have the right qualifications to have it?" "Am I righteous enough to have it?" "Have I fulfilled my calling well enough to have it?" "Have I repented enough to have it?" "Do others in authority recognize my worthiness?" Etc.

And the third one is...

"Do I Have a Right To It?"

Having The Right is a Rules issue.
This can mean things like, "Is it fair for me to have it?" "Am I justified in "having" it?" "Do I hold the right position to have it?" "Do I hold the right authority to have it?" "Do the right people acknowledge my right to it?" "Do I have the legal right to claim it?" "Do I have the proper credentials?" "Am I following the law here?" Etc.

These three, "Do I deserve it? Am I worthy of it? Do I have a right to it?" are all qualifying beliefs people have about themselves.

What's more, they may be invested in these beliefs which is a lot of energy. They tend to be hidden just out of sight where they can cause your manifestation efforts to fail. I add them here just so you can be aware.

If you feel that you have any of these beliefs, do the method and let go of them because like any thought, each one produces an emotion that can be released with the method.

If you feel "It's not OK" for you to just let them go, do The Core

Method on that first. Then let go of your hidden qualifiers.

One More Thing:

Sometimes people will take David Farragut's attitude of "Damn the Torpedoes, Full Steam Ahead!" and force themselves past all this qualification nonsense and try to make things happen no matter what.

This means they may use their "will power" to ignore all the different emotions they may feel along the way and bring their chosen goal or thing into their life, no matter what. Congratulations. You did it. But beware.

You must understand that when you don't lay a strong emotional foundation within yourself by clearing out the "baggage" and deal with beliefs that are blocking your success properly, the energies of the beliefs you hold inside will, as they say, "Come back to bite you".

Remember the law? "Like Attracts Like".

Those negative energies you hold inside will surely come and take those wonderful things right back out of your life. In fact, you may have experienced this before.

You work really hard to accomplish something and maybe you succeed. Or maybe you're getting close. Then all of the sudden, it all begins to fall apart. Or it becomes such a pain you can't go on. Or something happens and it gets taken away from you.

This is not uncommon. Ignoring the signs along the way will set you up for failure. So do the work. Let go of the baggage and hidden qualifiers along with all other dark and negative energies you may have collected along the way in life.

Doing the method will set the stage properly for the good you want to pull in and you will enjoy it far more and for far longer.

The subconscious mind cannot remove anything from your life.

In other words, you can't focus on something you don't like about your life and expect the subconscious mind to be able to remove it from you. That's not how it works.

The reason for this is because consciously focusing on something, whether you want it or not, is how your subconscious mind knows what to bring into your life.

Your subconscious mind is a one way street.
It can add to your life.
But it can't take anything out.

Focusing on what you don't want does not convey the message, "remove this" to the subconscious. The subconscious mind only recognizes what you focus on and works to bring it in. It does not recognize the, "I don't want this..." part.

Remember the quote in the Bible, "The thing I have feared hath befallen me"? This is because even back then they realized "What you focus on, is what fills you up, is what shows up..." whether you want it or not.

In other words, constantly thinking, "I don't want to fail" is how you assure your failure because the subconscious mind, which is your connection to the Universe, only works to bring in the thing it recognizes. It doesn't recognize, "don't" or "no" or "stop", etc. The one "thing" it does recognize is "fail". It knows what that is and will bring it in because of your focus on it.

When you want to remove something from your life, you change your focus to what you *do want* and focus on that instead. In time, what you *don't want* will simply fade away because it's getting no energy.

Fill yourself with the thought of what you *do want*. Do the method on anything that is not in alignment with it. In time and with persistence, the subconscious mind will bring what you choose for yourself into your life.

The other that you didn't want will eventually fade away because it is no longer getting any of your attention. This is because "energy flows where attention goes".

Direct your energy toward what you choose for yourself and that's what the subconscious mind will work to bring into your life. That's how the subconscious mind works.

26

The Core Method and the Power of Your Beliefs

As you may know, our beliefs have a very powerful effect on our lives. They're also a very personal thing. If you believe you can, then you probably will. If you believe you can't, then you probably won't.

Do "your" beliefs go for everyone? Not likely. There will be a number of people who will agree with you… and a number who won't. The thing about beliefs is that most all people have some beliefs that are stopping them from living a better quality of life than they are now living.

In fact, you may be aware of a belief or three that you wish you didn't have because you know if you didn't have them, you'd be far better off in life. Especially when you see others do well in life in spite of what you believe.

Think of a belief you have that you wish you didn't have. Like maybe you believe you will get sick simply because it's the season for it.

Maybe you believe life is a struggle.

Maybe you believe you are unlucky in love.

Maybe you believe you're too old, or too broke, or too fat, or you have too many responsibilities or money is the root of all evil.

Maybe you believe you're not smart enough or you don't have enough time or you're not attractive enough or you don't deserve happiness or your stars are evil and the Universe is set against you or... I think you get the picture.

For now, just think of a belief you have that you wish you didn't and keep it in the back of your mind. I'll bring it up in the next section.

I'm about to tell you a little secret about your beliefs. If everything I've taught you up to this point is true at all, then it's also true about your beliefs.

Beliefs that stunt your growth and limit your life are what you might call "problems". Remember I said that all problems have two parts... the story – and the emotion the story generates?

Beliefs are the same. The story is recorded in memory. It has a beginning, middle and end. You can always tell the story. Same with beliefs. The emotion that story generates is just this nebulous energy that churns inside of you. Same with the nebulous energies of beliefs.

What's more, the energies of those beliefs are responsive to your intention, which is energy, through your awareness, which is energy. This means you have access to your beliefs and they are responsive to The Core Method.

The Core of Your Body Communicates With Your World

I call your awareness and the "core" of your body the "center of your life". Like all of your beliefs, your negative beliefs generate an energy that your center, your midline or "core" broadcasts out into your world as energy.

This energy exchange with your world is constantly going on day and night. It is a communication going on between your inner self or your "identity" and the world you live in.

You feel it when you meet someone you *instantly* like or instantly dislike.

You feel it when you enter a place you love or feel uncomfortable in.

This communication has the effect of organizing your world to match the energies of your beliefs because the law states... "Like Attracts Like".

This is why you will always find evidence that your beliefs are true... for you.

Now, think of that belief I had you look for in the last section. Remember?

Bring it to the front.

As you think of it, you can probably remember times when your life played it out and proved this belief is spot on for you, right? Perfect. You are about to learn how to change your negative beliefs in seconds.

Hey! Is this OK with you?

Make sure it is because there is a lot written and spoken that says this is hard to do. No... it's not. Not when you use The Core Method.

If you have a problem with these kinds of things being easy, realize that this is a belief. Do the method on that belief. Keep reading. I'm about to tell you how.

Release That Belief!

Whatever that belief is, hold it in your mind. Be aware of all that you have experienced that proves this belief is true for you. This is to get the intensity of the feeling or emotion up on the "zero" to "ten" scale.

Feel the emotion this belief brings up. Where is it on the zero to ten scale? Feel that intensity and make a mental note of it.

Next, notice what's missing. What does this belief cause you to want? Is it wanting control? Wanting approval? Or wanting safety?

When you get a sense of which is the greatest want, (for this example, let's say it's "wanting control") think the thought... "Wanting control" one time.

As you think this thought, direct your awareness into your "core", down low at your tailbone and bring your awareness up your spine or "core", up your neck and out the top of your head, all in about three seconds or so. Then, take a breath and relax.

Now, go back to the belief.

Replay all that made you believe it was true. Does it still feel as true as it did before? Where is it on the zero to ten scale? Has it come down?

If there is any of it left, do the method on the rest of it. Only takes a few seconds. Do it until you can think of that belief and feel completely neutral about it. No attachments, no aversions and resistance.

No beating yourself up for ever having had such a belief. Think of what you would do now that this belief is gone. Does it feel more possible now? Or if you wanted to stop believing something, does it feel like less of or not even a "thing" anymore?

You are changing your "identity".

Things you believe make you act and live according to what those things dictate to you. If you are ready to get rid of the dictators in your life, then use the method on all your beliefs that don't serve you.

Every. Single. One.

You see, when it comes to the good things in life, which do you believe is better... "wanting" them... or "having" them?

I'm betting "having" them is your preference. "Having" is a state of being... the "Magical State". The more negative beliefs you eliminate, the more good things you "have". This is how you live a life of Authentic Magic.

Part Six

27

Knowing What to Let Go Of is Crucial to Your Magic!

You have The Core Method now.

You know how to remove the blocks to your Magic. But like I said, this whole thing is like learning to play chess.

You can learn how in a few minutes, but getting good at the game takes time and experience. This means it takes knowing what to look for inside. That's why I'm adding all these different concepts and metaphors.

Reading this book not only teaches you how to do the method, it also makes you familiar with many of the things people deal with that block the Magic in their lives and don't realize that's what's happening.

By reading these concepts and metaphors, you can have a better understanding of what to look for when you focus your awareness into your own psyche and emotional layers.

Everything I have added here in these later pages is advanced elements of the method. Work on clearing these things out of your "identity" and you'll be feeling the Magic sooner rather than later.

Attachments and Aversions

Attachments are anything you want or expect to be a certain way or turn out a certain way. Be it people, things or events.

Aversions are things you are trying to avoid. Things you do NOT want to have happen. Ways you do NOT want people to act. Events you do NOT want to experience or have happen.

When you are attached to an outcome, you become emotionally rigid and stuck, maybe even desperate. You want the thing to happen or be a certain way. This means you have expectations.

Having expectations is not a problem. Being attached to them is. It means you get bent out of shape if your expectations are not met.

When you are trying to avoid some thing or event, or trying to keep people from being a certain way, your attempts will cause a lot of inner turmoil. Maybe even anxiety and fear.

People who are rigid and stuck in their ways or are desperately for or against something are generally no fun to be around. They can be edgy and impatient. Angry and demanding.

Being attached or averse to something means "nothing else will do". You have decided that there's one way "this thing" must go and nothing else will satisfy you. This is a good way to justify overreacting emotionally if what happens isn't satisfying, which actually makes one look emotionally immature.

The ego loves this reasoning because this is a good way to experience conflict and the ego loves conflict with yourself or anyone else and for any reason. It also loves to be "right".

Especially when you don't get what you're attached to or what you are trying to avoid comes about anyway. Because then you get to disapprove of the result or person or thing and then beat yourself up. Or disapprove of someone else and beat them up emotionally.

This is always a very unloving thing to do because your subconscious mind or "conscience" keeps score which is called karma. That's coming up.

The basic goal of Authentic Magic is self love and flow.

Calmness and inner peace. Allowing and gratitude.

These states open one up to those possibilities that can't be seen or experienced when you're stuck. One aspect of this is releasing attachments and aversions, both of which have a feeling to them. It's a stuck or rigid feeling. Maybe even a desperate or fearful feeling.

The Core Method is perfect for these feelings. You know the drill by now.

Feeling attached to something? Trying to avoid something? Feel the emotion.

What does it bring up? Wanting control, approval or safety?

Do the method and release attachments and aversions. Now, watch for things to turn out even better than you thought.

If it's still not going like you choose, notice the story.

Feel the emotion. What does it bring up?

Wanting control, approval or safety?

Do the method.

Keep doing the method until all is resolved. Then notice that you got there with a smile and with your peace of mind intact. Magic!

Resistance

Pushing or fighting against something or someone creates negative energy, and a lot of resistance. This is a lot of attention on something you don't want.

To begin with, it fills you up with the thing you're resisting. Remember? "What you focus on, is what fills you up, is what shows up"!

You have to put a lot of attention on something in order to resist it. And like I said earlier... "Energy Flows Where Attention Goes". Or was it the other way around? You know what? It works *both* ways!

Aversion is a form of resistance. And resisting something is a good way to keep it.

Ever hear the phrase, "What you resist, persists"?

This is the reason why this is true. Resistance is giving a lot of attention to what you don't want. Your deeper self doesn't get the, "don't want" part. It only gets the "subject" of your focus.

In other words, the only thing your deeper self is interested in is the subject and that's what it works to bring in. This is why it's so important to focus on what you *do* choose for yourself.

When you do this, your creative subconscious doesn't remove the thing you don't want. It just stops bringing it in and starts bringing in the thing you now choose instead.

And how do you let go of resistance? Treat it just like any problem... do the method.

Think of the story.
Feel the emotion.
What's that bring up? Wanting control, approval or safety?
Put that "wanting" into your core and bring it up and out the top of your head.
Take a breath and relax.
Go back to the story.
Feel it again. Does it still feel the same? Or is it reduced or gone now?
If there's any left, do the method again. Do it until you feel nothing for the story or resistance.

Karma

Finally. We're here.

A lot of people believe in Karma. I do too, but I don't believe in it the same way many people do. Some are afraid of karma. Some think of it as a weapon or justified punishment. That's why I pondered this concept and came up with my own ideas and realizations about it. I'll share them with you here. Maybe they will help.

I realize there are those who hold fast to the idea of karma, meaning, if you try to remove this idea from them, they may throw a lot of resistance at you.

It might even be like trying to change their religious or political views. HA! Like… "WHOA! HOLD ON THERE BUCKO! NOBODY GETS OUT OF THEIR KARMA! GOT IT?"

Yeah, trying to take away these people's belief in karma can create quite an upheaval for them. So I won't try to do that, but I will tell you some things I've gathered in my experience.

Karma is *energy* created by our thoughts, words and deeds.

Each and every one of us creates our own karma, and we all must take responsibility for it.

When we create the unbalanced energies of bad karma in our lives, it's our responsibility to bring balance back to those energies. We have to bring balance to *our own* bad karma.

Basically, that means "pay" for our bad karma by doing a lot of good in the world or suffering in some acceptable way. You know, like we have to "atone" for our sins.

What's more, people even believe we have bad karma from our past lives. It follows us because even though we have no memory of what we did, that energy stays with us until we balance it out because energy cannot be created or destroyed. It can only be changed.

Key Point: Karma, even bad karma, is *energy* and it can be changed.

So one of my questions was, "Who's keeping track of my karma?" A lot of people talk about it like God keeps track of it. You know, it's that whole… "God's gonna get you for that!" thing, right? Like some divine personage is keeping notes in a book called, "The Book Of Life".

I think some even call it the Akashic Records? It's like someone is responsible for keeping your divine personnel file up to date with all the stuff you think, say and do. Sound familiar? Yeah, people believe that.

So, I'm curious. There were primitive tribes long ago that practiced human sacrifice because it was part of their beliefs. If they felt good about or felt the need to sacrifice a person and a lot of other people agreed it was for a good reason, would they have bad karma for it?

I mean, the effects of their actions are that someone died. What's more, if the person to be sacrificed had the same beliefs, then there's a chance they went to their death willingly for the good of the tribe. And although there might be those who are sad, pretty much everyone agrees it was necessary and acceptable. Few had a moral problem with it!

If we are each responsible for the kind and quality of the karma we create, wouldn't that mean they created good karma for themselves... by killing someone? Hmmmmm.

Let's get this straight... there is no one keeping a file on us. God has not hired a secretary to keep notes in a book on our activities while we're here on Earth.

Nope.

The fact is, we each keep our own karma stored in our own bodies and minds. This system makes it very simple for God. No books or notes or secretaries. Like I said, karma is energy... just like an attitude or belief is energy. Memories are energy too.

Since energy has no dimensions and takes up no space, we can store a lot of karma in our minds and bodies. This works because we all have a subconscious mind that remembers everything we've said and done. It's all recorded in our own personal memory.

Remember all those stories from life that generate those emotions? Yeah, we are each subconsciously keeping track of our own karma in the form of our "stories" stored in our memories.

We all have a conscience. A moral compass based on our values, beliefs and self-image. Even primitive tribes have this. Whenever we do something that goes against any of that, our conscience keeps track of it. All of that is basically held or stored in our body, our deeper self and in our memory. That's our karma.

Not only that, but your conscience will give you a little kick in the gut for the bad things you do. You know, that feeling you get in your middle or "core" that kinda makes you wince cause you know you just did something your conscience believes is bad.

Yeah, that feeling.

No one else is responsible for keeping track of your karma and no one else is responsible for deciding which is bad karma and which is good karma. We each determine all of that for ourselves.

Now, if karma is energy and it's stored right inside of each one of us as the energies of our stories and emotions, then we have access to all of our karma.

Remember that a problem has two parts? The story and the emotion it generates? Do you get where I'm going with this? Yeah, as you work on yourself with The Core Method, you can also release the energies of your karma and eliminate it.

So my question to you is, "Are you OK with that?" Because if you aren't, do the method on that too! The story does not cause us to attract the balancing energies for our karma. But the emotion does. Eliminate the emotions of your stories with The Core Method and you eliminate your karma.

One last note about this subject... if you have a problem with letting go of your karma so easily, go back and read the section called, "It's not OK!" That should help.

Waiting For The Other Shoe To Drop

Is it possible to have it too good in life? Have you ever mentioned in a conversation how good you have it or some good thing you have coming and then feel like you need to knock on wood?

A silly superstition, right? We even chuckle as we do it, right? But you know what? Many people actually hold the idea that if things in life get too good, somethings bound to happen to mess it up or take it away and so they actually live in a secret fear that might happen. Sad, but true. Do you know anyone like that? Maybe intimately?

Guess what... I know it's just a kind of silly thing we do... but too often there's some grounds for being that way. Like somewhere along the way in life we picked up the idea that to have it too good in life is unfair to other people who don't have it so good and it would hurt their feelings if we mention our good life while they sit there suffering.

Maybe God frowns on those of us who do too well in life and have the audacity to mention it and now God must knock us back down so we remember to be humble.

Or what if speaking of the good in your life is like tempting the devil to come and screw around with you like Job of the bible? Or maybe you feel that talking about how good you have it is bragging or boastful and that's a sin or socially taboo. Are you catching my drift?

Want to know what having it too good in life is? It's a story! And stories generate emotions like the fear you might somehow lose the good stuff of your life.

I'm not saying go around and tell everyone how good you have it. I'm saying that if you are holding the fear that recognizing and appreciating the good in your life might cause you to lose it or you even get the feeling you need to knock on wood, do the method on that. I promise you, it will do you a whole lot more good than knocking on wood.

28

Closing Notes

If You Do The Method and Don't Notice a Change

Do not assume it did not work.

Yes, it did.

It worked on what you applied it to, but maybe what you applied it to was not the real problem after all. Ask more questions of yourself.

Maybe it's just a different way of saying or addressing it. Dig a little deeper by sitting quietly with the thought/emotion and let it tell you where to direct your awareness.

When you come up with it, apply the method again to the feeling your inner self directs you to, then feel what's left.

Here's an example of what I mean.

I read a story where a young boy of about ten years or so was still pooping in his pants at night as he slept, like a little baby. This was *extremely* embarrassing to him, to say the least.

Problem was, no amount of therapy or physical measures worked to stop this. It was still happening to the poor kid and it was slowly destroying him emotionally, as you can probably imagine.

Finally, out of desperation, his parents employed this one person who did energetic psychology (much like you're learning here) who had a more open mind about how to approach things.

Part of his approach was to have the kid announce out loud to the therapist what was really happening so they could both get right to the honest truth or emotion of the problem. Remember, all problems have two parts? The story and the emotion?

At first, the therapist was trying to be sensitive to the age of the kid. So he was using more appropriate language for his age. He would make up lines and have the kid say them. Things like, "I poop in my pants". Or, "I crap in my pants." "I mess in my pants." Etc. But none of that seemed to work. They all seemed to miss the mark.

That is until the practitioner decided to put aside the age appropriateness thing and get real honest. He looked the kid right in the eyes and told him to say this... "I SHIT in my pants!" And Holy Presto Chango!... the kid broke completely apart, the tears came and the healing happened! It was done!

That was it! That's exactly how the kid felt about it. And that's what his inner, deeper self needed to hear... the honest truth. After that little experience, it was all gone. The kid never had another night of embarrassment.

Later it was discovered that the kid had heard his parents discussing this problem in the other room on many occasions and that's the word they used. And being his parents, he felt they were telling it like it was. The honest truth.

That's why nothing else worked. In the presence of all those adults, this kind of language was never used. But this is what the kid needed... blunt adult honesty.

This is why I say if you don't feel a change, do not assume it didn't work. The method will always work when you address the issue in a straight forward, honest way.

This is because you are dealing with your subconscious mind and it only knows your truth. A lie or untruth will make you feel a weakness in your body. The truth will give you a strong feeling in your body. Do the method and clear what comes up.

If there's any of that feeling left, do it again. Control, approval or safety. Often our stories generate layered emotions. Anger covers fear which may cover guilt which may cover shame which... see what I mean?

Do the method on what it feels like and then do the next emotion. Do them in turn until you feel neutral and at peace about that story. It only takes seconds for each application and the results can be amazing.

Take the time every day to learn to pay special attention to your emotions down in your body. Be aware of them. Welcome them up! The negative ones want out! Use the method and give them your permission!

Stay focused on the feelings and emotions in your body, not the story in your head. Stay out of your head as you do this method, just "know" what story makes you feel bad then focus down in your body. Feel the emotion about that story and do the method. It doesn't take long to clear out a lot of "baggage" with The Core Method.

Do this method with every negative emotion that comes up about anything!

- The kids
- The wife/husband or significant other
- Driving in traffic
- The in-laws
- Teachers
- Old memories of trauma
- Anxiety about a future event
- Money problems
- A big, important meeting
- Speaking in public
- Making videos
- EVERYTHING!

Since it only takes seconds to do, you can work with lots of emotions very quickly. In fact, you can do six months of therapy in a half hour with this method! And the more you do it, the better it works.

You're building a new relationship between your head and your heart. They are communicating! Then you build "momentum". A powerful force for long term healing and emotional health and happiness. And this is how you make the Magic flow.

Make a new habit of doing this with yourself for five or ten minutes or more every day and you will become lighter and lighter. In fact, let this become a new and powerful habit!

The more you do it, the lighter you get and the better you feel and the more you accomplish! Soon you will begin to feel the natural calm and peace that dwells within your spirit all the time. It's actually there. True story.

The Magic Of The Core Method... Emotional Release!

When you feel bad about something, you can change how you feel about it in seconds by using the method to let go of "wanting" it to change so you can experience the feeling of "having" the change. This is how it works with feelings and emotions.

Why?

Because they are energy and they are changed by the proper application of effective energetic tools. What's more, the changes are immediate and lasting.

With the Law of Attraction, when you are experiencing the emotional state of "having" something, you increase the possibility exponentially that it can actually come into your experience. This means when you let go of "wanting" and experience the feeling of "having", you send a new and positive message to your deeper self that says...

"I Have It Now! I'm Complete"!

You've placed your order with the Universe. Now let it do its job. The "having" state is the Magical State! Whether you actually have the new thing or situation or not is irrelevant. That you *feel* like you have it means everything to your deeper self.

There's a confidence and calmness in owning the assumption that what you've chosen now belongs to you. It's the feelings of your emotions that your deeper self or subconscious mind responds to. When you experience the feeling of "having"", you experience wholeness and completion.

No matter what your outer circumstances may be, you have a feeling of success, of being a winner. And with the Law of Attraction, it's this feeling of wholeness that your subconscious mind responds to by conspiring with the Universe and attracting into your life what you now "feel" you "have" in order to make your inner picture and outer picture match!

And the "having" state is the Magical State! Whether you actually have the new thing or situation or not is irrelevant. When you "feel" like you have it, this means everything to your deeper self. There's a confidence and calmness in owning the assumption that what you've chosen now belongs to you.

You've placed your order. Now you have every "right" to expect it to show up. It's the feelings of your emotions that your deeper self or subconscious mind responds to.

When you experience the feeling of "having", you experience wholeness and completion. Regardless of what your outer circumstances may be, you have a feeling of success, of being a winner.

My Three Rules of Life

I've shared these three rules with many other people over the years and they have been appreciated. So I thought, why not share them here. I'm not expecting you to take them up and they are not part of The Core Method, but they might remind you of qualities you have which may help make things go a little easier in life when you hold them.

They are very simple rules based on respect for yourself and others, and should be self explanatory. If they aren't, meditate on them. I hope you will come to realize the depth and significance of each of them. Here they are...

- Rule #1 – I don't go where I'm not welcome.
- Rule #2 – I give others the space to be who they are, and not be who they are not.
- Rule #3 – I reserve the right to my opinion and my preference and I give others the same rights.

When you understand these rules, you'll see how they compliment each other and work together. I was not always such a happy guy. But with The Core Method and living by these rules, I have found a lot of peace in life. And the Magic does flow.

Authentic Magic

Magic has no attachments.
Magic has no aversions.
Magic disapproves of nothing.
Magic beats nothing up.
Magic resists nothing. Magic judges nothing.
Magic is not afraid because Magic believes in itself.
Magic is not angry, guilty, ashamed, or jealous.
It is not greedy or small minded or limited by anything.
The Magic of the human spirit can overcome any
problem the human condition can imagine or create.
Magic deserves everything, is worthy of everything
and has the right to everything.
Magic is mature and complete. Therefore it
lacks nothing and owns everything.
And the most Magical thing of all?
Magic is your natural state of being.
Magic is the calm and silent background of your life.
Magic is the reality of your own human spirit.
As you remove all that is negative and blinds you to the
world of possibilities that surrounds you right now,
you will come to realize what it means to
live a life of Authentic Magic.
You will be amazed every day at how wonderful life
really is, and can be, regardless of circumstances.
I wish this realization and life upon you
with all my heart. Therefore, so be it.

Magic or misery.

It's your life.

It's your choice.

You have the authority.

And now you have the method.

About the Author

Hi there! I'm Jim Shane.

A pretty ordinary guy born in Mesa, Az in 1950. I've lived a fairly average life with the typical and not so typical ups and downs. Work, marriage, kids, divorce, and now retired, single and loving it.

Early in life, a chance discovery made me aware that I had an inclination to know what makes people tick. What makes us the way we are and do the things we do. This put me on a path of self discovery and life change.

Along the way, I learned that there are some amazing ways to let go and heal the past. Simple methods that can make life a whole lot more enjoyable including ways to make the Law Of Attraction work to our favor. Ultimately, I discovered and developed The Core Method from all that I learned.

I discovered that by applying this method, my life improved beyond my own efforts. Things seemed to just happen for me. As I shared the method, other people's lives improved too. I came to call this kind of experience Authentic Magic. The magic of the human spirit.

My desire here is to share what I have learned. So I compiled it into this book to share a simple method so that you may be empowered to use this tool. When you do, you can let go of everything keeping you from your most amazing life and live your own life of Authentic Magic. That's my wish for you.

My Story of the Healing Hand

You may have noticed the image of the healing hand on the cover above my name. It's a replication of the image on the amulet I wear around my neck. It doesn't really have anything to do with The Core Method, at least not directly. It really only has significance to me. I've worn it for over twenty years. But I wanted it to be part of my effort to write this book because it has spiritual meaning to why I wrote it.

I bought it at the Arizona Renaissance Festival in February of 1999. There is a booth where you can get a one inch silver blank stamped on both sides with images of your choice. They do it by setting the blank in a holder directly beneath a very heavy weight suspended by a rope. They crank it up to a certain height and let it drop with a thud. You can often feel the ground shake when it hits. Very cool.

On the backside of mine is a Celtic knot representing my Irish heritage. But I always wear the healing hand facing out. I know it may be called other names by other people and groups, but this is what it means to me.

When people see it and ask me what it means, I always direct their attention to the spiral first. I tell them, "That's the spirit. Follow the line down around the bottom and it comes up and forms the hand. That's the physical. One line, one source. The spirit and the flesh are one. Or God is in us."

But I don't usually go into detail about how I really hold this symbol. The rest goes like this...

When referring to the path of life, it is common to speak of the "circle of life". I don't hold life as a circle. I hold it as a spiral. As we go around the spiral of life, we have experiences. That's the purpose of life... to have experiences.

As we go around having experiences, we may be spiraling up if the experiences are good, and we may be spiraling down if the experiences are not so good. It depends on how much one is paying attention to the life they are living.

Life presents us with experiences so that we may grow and mature spiritually. This physical world gives us that opportunity. Along the spiral path of life, there are experiences that are meant to help us grow in knowledge and wisdom. If we are noticing them, we tend to grow up the spiral. If we aren't paying attention, we may slip down the spiral. But that's not the end of it.

As we go around, if we miss an experience or bit of knowledge, it will likely be there the next time we come around. We may even have several opportunities to "get it". The good news is, each time we go around, we have other experiences that may prepare us to finally receive that bit of information the next time we encounter it. What's more, this is happening at every point all the way around the spiral. This means every day is an opportunity for one to grow.

The knowledge and wisdom one may gather as they go around the spiral path of life is meant to be shared with others. That's how they may have that experience or get that next bit of knowledge. Whether one knows it or not, we are here to help each other grow in knowledge and wisdom. Sharing what we know is how we help.

This book contains knowledge and wisdom I have gathered from my own spiral path. It is my hope that somehow, you will benefit from what's contained here so that your travels may take you up the spiral path to greater health, wealth and happiness and ultimately to the other greater goals you may hope for. It is also my hope that as you travel, you will share what you have learned. Others are being prepared everyday for what you might share. And it may just change their life for the better.

Apply what you learn here and you will be better able to travel up your spiral path and help others along your way. You will become a blessing to yourself and others. This is my hope for you.

Jim

More Testimonials

"Jim has shared some amazing skill building technology with me called CORE. It has done wonders in helping me to manage my emotions in areas where there has been difficulties doing so before. Kudos to Jim for developing this approach and being so willing to coach his friends in how to apply it to their lives. Thanks a million."

SRM Arizona

"Now Jim, I am a procrastinator... you need to know this about me. Not all the time but since I have ADD.. (I think) I do not like to do things until I feel I am calm and can give things my full attention. I was feeling down from coming home after our 3 day visit to Disneyland for my granddaughter's birthday. I did not feel at peace or at rest at the time I was reading your message (the shortened Core).. but just as I was reading it, I was doing it. So it was not a really good effort... I wanted to wait to tell you later if the effect lasted... and it did!!! I had no time to be in the right state of mind when I read your message on the new way for CORE I was feeling bad at that very moment. I did it in the quickest way I could without full effort... AND IT WORKED. It has been a few days now and I am still feeling good!!!"

EM California

"Hello Jim, I have been using your method, and I'm pleased to report I am getting positive results. I suffer from depression, post traumatic stress disorder, and chronic anxiety. I have been working hard for awhile now on overcoming the root of my issues. However, I have not been able to control my feelings in the moment I have been triggered. It was not until I began using your method that I could get clarity on a situation quickly enough before my emotions were triggered and I did or said something I regretted. I found using your method reduced my anxiety significantly when I used it during moments of feeling high anxiety. I was able to bring my anxiety level of 8 or 9 to a 3 or 2 in most situations. I also used The CORE Method when I was nearing a panic attack. I do not get these often but I do suffer from one every three weeks. I did

experience a panic attack approaching with an anxiety level of 10. I used your method, and within a minute I brought it down to a level 5, and then to a level 3. All in all, I found The CORE Method to be very effective when using it to reduce anxiety. I was able to turn problems around that triggered me quickly, and therefore approach them with more clarity. I would recommend this method to anyone to assist people in making decisions they feel good about. Thank you, Jim, for being in my life. With Love..."

TP Arizona

"I met Jim Shane during a very dark place in my life. I was having extreme panic attacks, anxiety, and depression due to being raped repeatedly. This trauma left me unable to do daily activities. Things that I enjoyed I was no longer able to do because my pain and fear of men and being trapped by any man threw me in a debilitating panic attack following weeks of depression that kept me in bed.

I couldn't even walk down the street. I couldn't stand to wear color on my skin. All my clothing I wore had to be black. Flashbacks, nightmares, and insomnia was now my new life. I was prescribed narcotics that left me sick to my stomach and foggy. I even had to change my job because I could no longer stand to work with men. I felt like the woman I was before had died and left me with this weak broken victim who hated and feared my life.

I no longer wished to be held back. I wanted a change but didn't know how. Nothing I tried seemed to be working. I worked with Jim using The Core Method, on my fear of being in public. This gave me tools that I have used in so many other situations in my life. Jim's Core Method allowed me to take back my power. Today... I am no longer scared of men. I do not take any narcotics. I am currently going back to school to become a female mechanic. My goal is to empower other women in the mechanic world. Everything that held me back no longer controls me. I love my life again. I am able to be an emotionally and physically available mom to my two incredible amazing boys. I don't allow my life to be controlled by my trauma. I am no longer broken or a victim...I am a strong warrior woman, a survivor. I choose to live my life to its fullest. I will forever be thankful for Jim Shane and showing The Core Method healing that I needed.

MO Arizona

"I read the Core Method PDF you sent me and did the work. I took a feeling that has been niggling at me for some time now, a feeling of not being good enough, of not being successful. When I use the Core Method, I always feel like it's an elevator. It seems to stop at certain floors for a few seconds (usually my heart or throat area). I'll often tear up there, or feel a strong flood of emotions. It feels right to stay on that 'floor' until they dissipate. Then I move on up through my head, though usually, the intensity of the feeling has already gone down. When I got to my heart area with that feeling of not being successful, for some reason I felt like a little girl not getting approval from my mom. I felt a big welling up of emotion, then a release, and yeah-by the time I went up into my head, it felt gone. Just reading your PDF, I'm again blown away by how easy the method is. "

FHDA Canada

(From a lady I worked with who used the method to help a friend in a belly dance class)

"I did a little bit of what you did with me (kinda) with L... yesterday. She was having a difficult time in our belly dancing class and was stressing about everyone watching her. She couldn't believe how easy it was and how much better she felt. Thank you again Jim for everything. "

MO About LT Arizona

"Jim is one of the most authentic, present and grounded men I know. He has crafted a method which simplifies all the overthinking into a fast and easy way to let it go and let it flow! I have known Jim for 10 years, and appreciate and enjoy sharing our time on Earth learning from and supporting each other while we love and support the people around us. Thank you for inviting me to help you bring this work to the world!"

AK Arizona

Resources

Books, People, and Helpful Things I Have Mentioned in this Book.

Books:
TNT: The Power Within You – 1932
by Claude M. Bristol (Author), Harold Sherman (Author)

Think and Grow Rich (Official Publication of the Napoleon Hill Foundation) Paperback – 1937 by Napoleon Hill (Author)

The Magic of Believing: The Classic Guide to Unlocking the Power of Your Mind
by Claude M. Bristol May 15, 2019

Psycho-Cybernetics: 1960 by Maxwell Maltz

The Power of Now: A Guide to Spiritual Enlightenment
by Eckhart Tolle Aug 1, 2004

The Secret (Feb 26, 2007)
by Rhonda Byrne (Author)

Urban Shaman
by Serge Kahili King Nov 15, 1990

Freedom from Fear Forever: The Acu-Power Way to Overcoming Your Fear, Phobias and Inner Problems
by James V. Durlacher | Jan 1, 1997

Bradley B. Nelson: Emotion Code : How to Release Your Trapped Emotions for Abundant Health, Love and Happiness (Paperback); 2007 Edition by Bradley B. Nelson | Jan 1, 1679

Feeling Is The Secret
by Neville Goddard Jan 20, 2015

Magic Eye: A New Way of Looking at the World
by N.E. Thing Enterprises Oct 5, 1993

Uberman: 2nd Edition: Go DEEP Down The Rabbit Hole, Learn Powerful Techniques For Creating The Life You Want... And Obliterate *Anything* That Stands In Your Way! Paperback – February 19, 2020 by Jason Mangrum (Author)

Web resources:
- Thought Field Therapy (TFT) - https://www.goodtherapy.org/learn-about-therapy/types/thought-field-therapy
- Release Technique - https://www.releasetechnique.com/
- Sedona Method - https://www.sedona.com
- The Silva Mind Control Method - https://www.silvamethod.com/
- Vadim Zeland - Reality Transurfing - https://zelands.com/
- BSFF (Be Set Free Fast) - https://www.besetfreefast.com/
- Art Of Neutrality - https://chineseenergetics.com/
- Dr. Wayne Dyer - https://www.drwaynedyer.com/
- Emotional Complex Clearing (ECC) - https://www.ecctherapy.com/ On this ECC website, scroll down a bit and you'll see two preview videos, "Jim Before" and "Jim After". Dr. May doing his work with me. It was Amazing! These videos are from 1998 when I really began to delve into Energetic Psychology.
- Elma Mayer, Now Healing - https://www.nowhealing.com/
- Emotional Freedom Techniques (EFT)- https://www.emofree.com/
- Tony Robbins - https://www.tonyrobbins.com/
- Erhard Systems Training (EST) - http://www.erhardseminarstraining.com/
  I went through the Lifespring Training which came out of EST - no longer available.
  https://en.wikipedia.org/wiki/Lifespring
- Kam Yuen and his "Yuen Method" -https://yuenmethod.com/
- Psycho Cybernetics - https://www.psycho-cybernetics.com/

Stay Connected

FB Page - @TheCoreMethodCoaching
You Tube - The Core Method Coaching

Made in the USA
Columbia, SC
08 July 2022